File on
GENET

Compiled by Richard C. Webb

Methuen Drama

Contents

A Methuen Drama Book

First published in 1992 as a paperback original
by Methuen Drama, Michelin House,
81 Fulham Road, London SW3 6RB,
and distributed by HEB Inc., 361 Hanover Street,
Portsmouth, New Hampshire 03801-3959, USA

Copyright in the compilation
©1992 by Richard C. Webb
Copyright in the series format
©1992 by Methuen Drama
Copyright in the editorial presentation
©1992 by Simon Trussler

Typeset in 9/10 Times by
L. Anderson Typesetting,
Woodchurch, Kent TN26 3TB

Printed in Great Britain

ISBN 0 413 65530 X

A CIP record for this book
is available from the British Library

The theatre is, by its nature, an ephemeral art: yet it is a daunting task to track down the newspaper reviews, or contemporary statements from the writer or his director, which are often all that remain to help us recreate some sense of what a particular production was like. This series is therefore intended to make readily available a selection of the comments that the critics made about the plays of leading modern dramatists at the time of their production — and to trace, too, the course of each writer's own views about his work and his world.

In addition to combining a uniquely convenient source of such elusive *documentation*, the 'Writer-Files' series also assembles the *information* necessary for readers to pursue further their interest in a particular writer or work. Variations in quantity between one writer's output and another's, differences in temperament which make some readier than others to talk about their work, and the variety of critical response, all mean that the presentation and balance of material shifts between one volume and another: but we have tried to arrive at a format for the series which will nevertheless enable users of one volume readily to find their way around any other.

Section 1, 'A Brief Chronology', provides a quick conspective overview of each playwright's life and career. *Section 2* deals with the plays themselves, arranged chronologically in the order of their composition: information on first performances, major revivals, and publication is followed by a brief synopsis (for quick reference set in slightly larger, italic type), then by a representative selection of the critical response, and of the dramatist's own comments on the play and its theme.

Section 3 offers concise guidance to each writer's work in non-dramatic forms, while *Section 4*, 'The Writer on His Work', brings together comments from the playwright himself on more general matters of construction, opinion, and artistic development. Finally, *Section 5* provides a bibliographical guide to other primary and secondary sources of further reading, among which full details will be found of works cited elsewhere under short titles, and of collected editions of the plays — but not of individual titles, particulars of which will be found with the other factual data in Section 2.

The 'Writer-Files' hope by striking this kind of balance between information and a wide range of opinion to offer 'companions' to the study of major playwrights in the modern repertoire — not in that dangerous pre-digested fashion which can too readily quench the desire to read the plays themselves, nor so prescriptively as to allow any single line of approach to predominate, but rather to encourage readers to form their own judgements of the plays in a wide-ranging context.

Jean Genet, canonized by Sartre and demonized by those who saw the Black Mass being celebrated in his work, provoked a stronger critical response by far than the French 'absurdists' who were his contemporaries: and the reviewers who repudiated what they understood his plays to be saying drew upon a vocabulary of disgust which had seldom been unleashed since Ibsen's *Ghosts*. There, of course, syphilis was used as a dramatic metaphor: but in the worlds of Genet's plays, vehicle and tenor, signifier and signified, are less readily separable, and sometimes merge altogether. Physical disguise, like its verbal counterpart, does not 'stand for' something else, but is part of the experience it encompasses.

It is perhaps a pity that the direct political involvement of Genet's later years never found its dramatic form — indeed, that his genius found little dramatic expression at all beyond that sudden burst of energy of the mid-1950s. Yet for all his concern with the ritual and ceremonial qualities of theatre, Genet's plays have profound political implications — here, sexuality is not sublimated in the quest for power, but is the expression of power itself. As early as 1961, when many critics were ill-at-ease with what they understood as Genet's reduction of all human experience to an erotic basis, Kenneth Tynan (as recorded on p. 60-1) had thus already understood 'the recurrent Genetic idea that all human relationships are power relationships. There are those who dominate and those who are dominated.'

Genet in his time was almost alone among playwrights in this ability to dramatize not merely the power of the erotic, but the erotics of power. Feminist criticism, which has since converted such perceptions almost into commonplaces, has in so doing arguably also diminished for today's audiences the significance of Genet's dramatic vision. Not that it is uncommon for critics who were apparently shocked by a play's first production subsequently to dismiss a revival as old hat: and homophobia, which in the 1950s and beyond might be happily declared with coy references to 'perversity', must now be more covertly indulged. Yet there is no longer the sense, expressed in many of the early reviews here reprinted, that, for better or worse, Genet's plays get to the very core of our beings: they begin to be viewed, rather, as products of a particular historical moment. It remains to be seen whether they emerge from our own historical moment merely as eccentric symptoms of mid-century hang-ups — or as classics which convey a universal truth in terms of the hidden obsessions of their times.

Simon Trussler

Since Genet's death various studies have appeared which challenge the version of his early life as recounted by Sartre in his Saint Genet: comédien et martyr *(1952). The diaries and letters of people associated with Genet have also begun to appear, adding detail to what we know about him. This chronology attempts to put some order into recent (and continuing) revelations.*

1910   Genet is born on 19 December at a public clinic in Paris to Camille Gabrielle Genet; his father is unknown.

1911   On 28 July his mother abandons him to the care of the public authorities. Two days later he is placed with Eugénie and Charles Régnier in Alligny-en-Morvan.

1922   Genet takes his First Communion on 4 June.

1923   On 15 July Genet's successful school career is marked by his gaining the 'good' grade in his first school certificate.

1924   In October, Genet is transferred to the Ecole d'Alembert, a residential school for the more gifted children in care where they can specialize in joinery or printing. Genet runs away and is found in Nice on 10 November. The director of the school notes that Genet has shown signs of being affected by reading adventure stories and has expressed the desire to escape ever since arriving at the school. He is returned to the care of the public authorities in Paris.

1925   In the first week of April, Genet is placed with the blind composer René de Buxeuil in Paris. In November he is found guilty of misappropriating 180 francs of the composer's money (Sartre places this theft earlier, while Genet is still with his foster parents). He is taken for observation and psychiatric tests to the Hôpital Henri-Rousselle in Paris. The results state that Genet suffers from a certain degree of mental weakness and instability. Genet has indicated that it was during his stay at the hospital that he became aware of his homosexuality in an albeit innocent incident involving an exchange of sweets with a fellow patient called Divers. Genet is moved to a Paris hostel for the protection of young people in moral danger.

1926   On 9 February Genet runs away from the hostel. He is arrested in Marseilles two days later and is returned to Paris.

Genet continues to escape from institutions until, in May, he arrives at Mettray, an agricultural penal colony near Tours. Genet has identified Mettray as the place where he first experienced the emotions that led him to writing. He always refers to Mettray in affectionate terms.

1929   On 1 March Genet enlists in the army for a two-year term.

1930   On 4 February Genet arrives in Beirut with his regiment and is stationed in Damascus. This is his first experience of the Middle East, which is to occupy his attention in the later years of his life. He returns to Avignon on 25 December.

1931   Genet possibly makes his first journey to Spain, before enlisting in Bayonne for a second two-year term in June. He is posted to Meknes in Morocco. For a three-month period, he acts as secretary to the commanding officer in Midelt. Morocco, too, is to play an important role in his later life.

1933   Genet goes to Paris, where he visits André Gide, having apparently already read *L'Immoraliste* and *Les Nourritures terrestres*. This is the first documented contact Genet has with the established literary world. He plans to travel to North Africa. A letter to Gide, dated 12 December, finds Genet penniless in Barcelona. It is almost certainly from this period that the experiences related in *Journal du voleur* are taken.

1934   In April Genet enlists for three years, and is posted to Toul with the 22nd Regiment of the Algerian Infantry. He reads Dostoyevsky, issues of *La Nouvelle Revue française*, and corresponds with the writer André Suarez, requesting copies of an out-of-print collection of poems and other works.

1935   On 15 October, Genet signs up for a further four years to run from the end of his present period of service. He is transferred to Aix-en-Provence to join the renowned Moroccan Colonial Infantry. Genet never did join the Foreign Legion, as reported by Sartre. This regiment resembled it and rivalled it in prestige.

1936   Genet deserts. After working in a transport company in Nice, he crosses the border to Italy in July, using false papers. A year-long journey across and around Europe begins: Albania, Yugoslavia, Italy again, Austria, Czechoslovakia, Poland, Germany, and Belgium. Elements of this journey are recounted in *Journal du voleur*.

1937 From December the previous year until May, Genet is resident in Brno. He helps support himself by giving French lessons to the wife of a rich industrialist, Anne Bloch, who is a friend of Lily Pringsheim. Correspondence from the period paints a picture of a highly literary and literate Genet whose only luggage was a briefcase containing manuscripts and writing materials. Genet returns to Paris in July. From September there begins a series of misdemeanours (petty thefts, false or faulty papers, travelling without a ticket) and lengthening prison sentences which stretch over the next several years.

1941 Through his acquaintance with Jean Decarnin, Genet works as a *bouquiniste* on the banks of the Seine.

1942 *Notre-Dame des fleurs* is probably begun in prison in January; a play, *Héliogabale*, and some film scenarios are reportedly already in manuscript form. In October a limited edition of 100 copies of *Le Condamné à mort* is in circulation. The edition was printed at Fresnes prison, probably at Genet's own expense. It is dated September. This marks the start of an intensely creative period. In the next four years Genet is to produce (if not publish) all his major novels, and other texts follow.

1943 On 7 February, Genet meets Jean Cocteau for the first time. Cocteau has already been impressed by *Le Condamné à mort*. The following evening, Genet reads an unpublished poem, *Le Boxeur endormi*, to Cocteau and his circle. He leaves Cocteau the manuscript of *Notre-Dame des fleurs*. Cocteau is a very influential promoter of Genet's work. Genet is to stay connected with Cocteau's circle until 1949. On 1 March, Genet signs his first publishing contract, which lists in addition to the works cited: two novels, *Le Mystère des enfants des anges* (first title for *Miracle de la rose*) and *Journal du voleur*, and no less than five plays, *Journée castillane*, *Héliogabale*, *Persée*, *Pour la Belle* (which will become *Haute surveillance*), and *Les Guerriers nus* (originally a film scenario). In November, Marc Barbezat agrees to publish *Miracle de la rose*, and *Spectre du coeur* (first title of *Pompes funèbres*) is begun and destroyed.

1944 In letters from prison dated March, there is mention for the first time of the poems *La Galère* and *Marche funèbre*. *Spectre du coeur* is taken up again. With his release in May, Genet's periods in prison come to an end. Back in Paris, he meets Simone de Beauvoir and Jean-Paul Sartre. An unnamed film project is referred to in letters. In September the full text of *Notre-Dame des fleurs* is published in a limited edition by Paul Morihien, backed by Jean Cocteau.

1945 In March, Marc Barbezat publishes *Chants secrets* (containing *Le Condamné à mort*, *Dédicace*, and *Marche funèbre*). *La Galère*, and extracts from *Miracle de la rose* and *Pompes funèbres*, appear in journals. A five hundred page novel (probably *Querelle de Brest*) is alluded to in letters, as are two plays, *Splendid's* and *Don Juan*. There remains three months of work to do on *Journal du voleur*. *Haute surveillance* is completed.

1946 In February Genet writes to Barbezat concerning an expanded collection of poems entitled *Un Chant d'amour* which is to contain: *A M. Pilorge*, *Condamné à mort*, *Marche funèbre*, *A Lucien Sénémaud*, *Un Chant d'amour*, *La Galère*, *Guy I et II*, *La Parade*, *Le Flic*, *Secret*, *Voleur I et II*, *Boxeur*. The title poem appears in a literary magazine in the Spring, which also sees a collectors' edition of *Miracle de la rose*. *Querelle de Brest* is completed. The July issue of *Les Temps modernes*, edited by Sartre, includes an extract of *Journal du voleur*. In May, Genet is condemned to two years imprisonment which is commuted to ten months. It is this sentence which prompts Sartre, Cocteau, and other literary figures to mount a defence of Genet, leading to a presidential pardon in 1949.

1947 *Haute surveillance* appears in a literary journal in February. It is reported that Jean-Louis Barrault is to put it on in the coming season. *Les Bonnes* is performed on the stage of the celebrated director Louis Jouvet in April. The text is published the following month in a magazine; another version, described as the 'true version', is sent to Barbezat in November. Genet is awarded a literary prize (*Le Prix de la Pléiade*) for these two plays. A playscript entitled *Frolic's* (assumed to be a variant title for *Splendid's*) is announced, along with a film, *La Révolte des anges noires*, on his childhood, and a novel, *Promis à la veuve*, a celebration of an executed friend. Away from the theatre, limited editions of *Pompes funèbres*, *Querelle de Brest*, and the poem *La Galère* are published.

1948 In May, the ballet *Adame Miroir* is performed by Roland Petit's fashionable company in Paris. In July, Cocteau and Sartre publish the text of the letter sent to President Auriol pleading for a pardon for Genet who, it is feared, runs the risk of banishment for his repeated past convictions. August sees the publication of a limited edition of *Les Poèmes* which includes the new work *Le Pêcheur du Suquet*. In December, Genet writes to Barbezat that he will be sending the definitive version of *Splendid's* in a fortnight.

1949 *Haute surveillance* is performed in Paris in February, the month of the publication of the banned radio text, *L'Enfant criminel*. Gallimard begins publishing Genet with *Haute surveillance* and *Journal du voleur*. Bernard Frechtman produces the first English translations of Genet's work: an extract of *Journal du voleur* and *Our Lady of the Flowers*. In August Genet is granted a Presidential pardon. After 1949 Genet appears to experience a creative block. Very few new substantial works are forthcoming until the rush of dramatic works in the mid 1950s.

1950   From April to June Genet makes the homo-erotic film *Un Chant d'amour*. He produces two short texts of artistic appreciation: *Lettre à Léonor Fini* and *Grec* (on Jean Cocteau).

1951   Gallimard publishes the second volume of his *Oeuvres complètes*. An untraced text, *Les Beaux Gars*, is announced. A substantial film scenario, *Mademoiselle ou les feux interdits*, is read by Henri Chapier.

1952   Genet goes to Greece, a country to which he often returns. As the first volume of Genet's *Oeuvres complètes*, Gallimard publishes Sartre's study *Saint Genet: comédien et martyr*, which refers to a vast work called *La Mort*. This is to incorporate a cycle of seven plays. It is unclear what has become of this project. A film project is begun with the Italian director Decimo Christiani, but *Le Bagne* is never to be produced. A theoretical political work, *Tentative de Compréhension du Communisme*, never appears in *La Nouvelle Revue française* as announced. Genet is reported to have destroyed the manuscript of *Frolic's* (or *Splendid's*), along with everything he has written in the last five years. In November, *Les Bonnes* (performed in French) is the first Genet production on the London stage.

1953   The third volume of his *Oeuvres complètes* appears.

1954   'La lettre à Pauvert', Genet's first commentary on the theatre, is printed in a volume containing two versions of *Les Bonnes*. The play is performed in January following the version not directed by Jouvet in 1947. The first American edition of the play is published with *Deathwatch*, in translations by Bernard Frechtman. The latter is also responsible for the first complete English translation of *The Thief's Journal*, which is published in Paris. A text on homosexuality, *Fragments*, appears in *Les Temps modernes*. This could be part of an essay on homosexuality entitled *Enfers*, announced by the publisher Pauvert. It may also be part of the untraceable *La Mort*. Genet is reported to have contemplated suicide during these uncreative years.

1955   Genet sees the Peking Opera in Paris. He travels with his friend Abdullah. He is reported to have signed a manifesto criticizing French colonialism. In May, *The Maids* is the first production of a Genet play in New York. In letters towards the end of the year, it becomes clear that Genet has entered another period of intense creativity, this time devoted to the theatre: he writes of having completed *Elle* (also called *Le Pape*) and *Le Balcon*. *Les Nègres* is being corrected. *Querelle de Brest* is translated into German, but is banned.

1956   By February, *Le Bagne* is in Barbezat's possession. In the same month Genet refers to 'the play about the Arab'; by June, Barbezat has seen the first draft; in September it is referred to as *Les Paravents*; it is nearly finished by December. Meanwhile, Genet renames *Les Nègres* as *Football*, and the fifteen-scene version of *Le Balcon* is published. Genet travels to see *The Maids*, the first English-language production of one of his plays, in London. Seizure of his novels by Customs and Excise officers in December leads to questions in the House of Commons.

1957   *The Balcony* is published and performed in London. *Splendid's* is to be staged in Paris. In letters in September, *Les Fous* is mentioned; *Les Paravents* is said to be finished. The text on the art of tight-rope walking (inspired by Abdullah) and the appreciation Alberto Giacometti appear in literary magazines.

1958   Genet spends at least the first half of the year in Corsica and Greece with Abdullah. *Les Nègres* is published and is read by Roger Blin. *Les Paravents* is still being revised. A first appreciation of Rembrandt is printed in the widely circulating *L'Express*.

1959   Genet continues to spend time in southern Europe, mainly Greece, from where he is reported to be directing *Les Nègres* by telephone. Blin's production opens in October. There are press announcements referring to a play, *La Mère* (an alternative title for *Les Paravents*), and to the seven-play cycle again.

1960   Genet is still spending time in Greece. *The Balcony* opens in New York in February, and in May Peter Brook directs it in Paris. A revised version in nine scenes is published with a short commentary by Genet. *Ça bouge encore* (another title for *Les Paravents*) is sent to the actress manager Marie Bell. *The Blacks* appears in English. Genet's plays are now being produced throughout Europe.

1961   Genet is still in Greece much of the time. *Les Paravents* is published; a truncated version is performed in Berlin. *The Blacks* has its premiere in New York; a production with an all-white cast in Amsterdam meets with the author's disapproval. Genet's intense period of published dramatic writing comes to an end. There follows a silence, apart from some revisions, notes on the theatre, and cultural texts.

1962   Genet is acquitted of obscenity in the German courts; *Our Lady of the Flowers* and *Querelle* are allowed to be published. Another version of *Le Balcon* appears with notes on its production by Genet. *The Screens* is printed in New York.

1963   Genet's popularity grows worldwide. In March, Joseph Strick's film of *The Balcony* is released in the USA. A contract is signed with Barbezat for an elusve text, *La Fée*. Genet refuses permission for a white production of *Les Nègres* by a Polish company.

1964   Genet grants his major interview to *Playboy*. Peter Brook's experimental RSC company perform a workshop production of the first twelve scenes of *The Screens*.

1965   Genet's close friend, the racing driver Jacky Mafia, is killed in a racing accident. Genet himself is refused an American visa on 'moral grounds'. *Miracle of the Rose* is published in England and the USA. A revised, 'definitive' version of *Haute surveillance* is edited by Gallimard. An American film of *Deathwatch* comes out. Work starts on location for Tony Richardson's film, *Mademoiselle*, based on Genet's filmscript.

1966   Amid great controversy in April, Roger Blin directs *Les Paravents* in Paris. Simultaneously the notes sent by Genet to Blin during rehearsals are published. In May, *Mademoiselle* is shown at Cannes. *La Rafale* (probably a variant title for *Le Bagne*) is announced. Almost simultaneously, the ban on *Miracle of the Rose* is being lifted in Australia; the original, uncut version of *Notre-Dame* is republished; *Querelle* is appearing in England; and Genet's film, *Le Chant d'amour*, is condemned as pornographic in California. Genet himself is rumoured to have become involved with the Zengakuren protesters in Japan.

1967   The press reports in May that Genet has suffered a heart attack induced by brandy and sleeping pills. It is possible that this is a suicide attempt following the suicide of Abdullah and also Frechtman (after some acrimonious litigation). Two texts appear: a discussion of Rembrandt curiously alongside an incident on a train and a collection of thoughts on art, death, and the theatre and their places in modern life.

1968   Genet becomes a public figure, associating himself with the students at the Sorbonne in May, and in August with the protesters at the Democratic Convention in Chicago. He writes an article in support of Daniel Cohn-Bendit's ideas on education; his published accounts of events in Chicago are virulent attacks on American society. He drafts a study in which he questions the notion of ownership in literary and dramatic creation. From 1968 Genet abandons literature in favour of political action and writing, supporting the Black Panthers, Baader-Meinhoff, and the Palestinians. The fourth volume of his *Oeuvres complètes* appears.

1969   Genet begins his involvement with the Black Panthers. Victor Garcia directs his acclaimed production of *Les Bonnes* in Barcelona.

1970   Genet is to be seen occupying the employers' headquarters in Paris in protest against the death of five Arab workers; he is arrested during a protest against developers who wish to evict two old men and demolish their house. He undertakes a speaking tour on behalf of the Black Panthers which culminates in his May Day Speech at Yale. Articles by him on the Panthers appear in *Le Nouvel Observateur* as well as in the black underground press in America. He writes the preface to *Soledad Brother: the Prison Letters of George Jackson*. He becomes involved with the cause of the Palestinians.

1971   Genet is the author of the preface to *L'Assassinat de Georges Jackson*. His text accompanies a photographic study of the Palestinians. In November, Genet is expelled from Jordan.

1972   Genet returns to the Middle East, to Beirut, and is deported. He demonstrates at Versailles after the death in custody of an immigrant. He returns to New York to help defend Black Panthers on trial.

1974   His declaration on the rights of immigrants is broadcast on France Culture. He uses this issue in newspaper articles to attack President Giscard d'Estaing. An article by him on Palestinian women appears in *Le Monde diplomatique*.

1975   Genet gives his most detailed interviews to the German author Hubert Fichte; he in turn interviews Angela Davis, the black activist. He refuses an official prize for his film *Un Chant d'amour* on the grounds that to accept it from the Minister of Culture, Michel Guy, would compromise his position and his life's work.

1976   A film project, *La Nuit venue*, is begun. In spite of two years work, the film is never completed.

1977   Genet writes the introduction to a collection of letters and articles by the German terrorist organization, the Red Army Faction (Baader-Meinhoff). An edited version is published by *Le Monde*.

1979   An interview with the author Tahar Ben Jalloun concerning new legislation affecting the rights of immigrants appears in *Le Monde* and is translated in *The Guardian Weekly*. The fifth volume of his *Oeuvres complètes* comes out.

1982   Genet is the subject of a video cassette directed by Antoine Bourseiller in which he speaks at length about his life, work, and inspiration. Fassbinder makes his film of *Querelle*. In September Genet witnesses the Israeli invasion of Lebanon. He is to spend much time with the Palestinians until his death.

1983   Genet goes to Vienna to publicize the cause of the Palestinians; he publishes an article about the Chatila camp, and begins to write his final work, *Le Captif amoureux,* an intimate account of the struggles of the Palestinian people. The socialist Minister of Culture, Jack Lang, awards Genet a National Prize in recognition of his work.

1986   On 15 April, while correcting the proofs of *Le Captif amoureux*, Genet, suffering from throat cancer, falls in a Paris hotel and dies. He is buried at Lavache in Morocco.

a: Major Plays

Deathwatch (Haute surveillance)

Written: begun before Jan. 1944, under title of *Pour la Belle*;
completed by Dec. 1945 with new title, *Préséances*.

First production: Théâtre des Mathurins, Paris (dir. Jean
Marchat and Jean Genet).

First American production: Pieta Theater, Cambridge,
Massachusetts, March 1957 (dir. Stephen Aaron).

First British Production: Arts Theatre, London, 25 June 1961
(dir. Ronald Hayman).

Major revivals: Theater East, New York, 9 Oct. 1958 (dir. Leo
Garen); Théâtre Recamier, Paris, 15 Sept. 1970 (dir.
Arcady); Young Vic, London, 13 April 1972 (dir. Frank
Dunlop, in a double-bill with *The Maids*); East Fourth
Street Theater, New York, Sept. 1975 (dir. Joann Green);
Le Coupe-Chou (Beaubourg), Paris, Feb. 1978 (dir. Claude
Mathieu); Foco Novo at the Repertory Studio Theatre,
Birmingham, and on tour, Feb. 1985 (dir. Nigel Williams);
Royal Shakespeare Company at The Pit, Barbican, London,
12 Oct. 1987 (dir. Gerard Murphy and Ultz, in a double-
bill with *The Maids*).

First published: in the review *La Nef*, No. 28 (March 1947),
p. 94-112, and No. 29 (April 1947), p. 92-112; the 1949
Gallimard edition shows textual variants; the revised 1965
'édition définitive' is reprinted in the *Oeuvres complètes*
with a note requesting that the play not be performed again;
it is reported that the director Michel Dumoulin asked
Genet to revise the play in 1985.

Translations: by Bernard Frechtman as *Deathwatch*, based on
the 1949 prompt copy (New York: Grove, 1954); there
followed an 'acting version which supersedes the published
text' (London: Faber, 1961); by David Williams, a new,
translation for the Foco Novo production, unpublished;
by David Rudkin, combining elements from 1949 text to
supplement 1954 Frechtman translation, for RSC
production, unpublished.

---

*Green Eyes, Lefranc, and Maurice share a prison cell
where they are trapped in a spiral of increasingly*

passionate confrontations, fired by their jealousy, envy, and rivalry. *Green Eyes* is the murderer of a young woman and is awaiting his fate in an aloof, self-possessed way. He deals with the guards and is in contact with the absent Snowball, the black king of the criminals. Lefranc, who himself aspires to the god-like, solitary status of the heroic criminal, is the writer of *Green Eyes's* love letters. He exploits this position to aggravate *Green Eyes* and to antagonize Maurice, his boyish accolyte. Lefranc taunts Maurice for his fawning, unrequited adoration of the murderer; Maurice goads the dour Lefranc with his lack of stature and the pettiness of his crimes. The play reaches its climax as Maurice exposes the spuriousness of Lefranc's contacts with the great criminals, a spuriousness symbolized in a fake tattoo. Lefranc strangles Maurice only to be faced with *Green Eyes's* utter contempt for this impassioned act. Lefranc is left to contemplate his own isolation.

[From its first production, Genet's play has provoked widely contrasting appreciations. Critical opinion divides most fundamentally over the question of whether Genet's writing has universal import or whether it is the private scribbling of an abject pariah. Particularly in France, this debate is entered into with almost unrestrained passion.]

The themes are foul. The tone is loathsome. . . . For forty-eight minutes, which seem like twenty-four hours, we are confronted with squalour in its most unadulterated form. A single word struck me as I watched: filth, . . . filth raised to the level of philosophy. Don't let's speak of eloquence nor dramatic force: it's a meditation on depravity, examined and handled with a supremely unpleasant smugness by an author who, I imagine, revels in observing those who are rotten to the core. Perhaps there will be those who will speak of poetry. Don't believe a word of it. Yes, there is writing, but of the worst sort, the type that touches rotting bodies and leprous minds.

We have had enough of these smells from the sewer, these self-satisfied stenches, these intellectual latrines!

Jean-Jacques Gautier, *Figaro*, 4 March 1949

It's been a long time since I can remember having seen or heard something as repulsive, as fundamentally unpleasant as this piece of high-blown nonsense which aims to prove the nobility, the dignity, and the glamour of crime.

Roger Belluc, *Revue de la Méditerranée*, VII, No. 3 (May-June 1949)

You do not think of laughing at this diseased display which is picked over delightedly by the author, like a tramp rummaging through a dustbin.

Guy Lerclerc, *L'Humanité*, 12 March 1949

[The author] goes round in circles within the cell of a vice from which literary creation cannot help him to escape, since he cannot conceive of anything beyond the barbed wire of this tiny, cursed world.

François Mauriac, 'Le Cas Jean Genet', *Figaro littéraire*, 26 March 1949

Here, trapped in a closed circuit, Genet continues with the extra-ordinary, narcissistic fantasy of *Our Lady of the Flowers*, without ever leaving the concentration camp of his own obsessions.

Matthieu Galey, *Nouvelles littéraires*, 24 Sept. 1970

[Genet's defenders have expressed themselves in equally colourful terms.]

Green Eyes's appalling yet beautiful dance, the scene when Lefranc strangles Maurice, and the desperate, romantic sincerity of the appeal to misfortune in the final lines of the poetic drama, disturb without ever gratifying. We are told to think that there is as much deception, vanity, childishness, and despair in the exceptional world of the criminal as there was possibly in the court of Louis XIV. We are made to believe that all specialists, whatever their specialty, share the same mannerisms and obsessions. . . . We are left with the certain belief that poetry can save, justify, and explain everything.

Jacques Lemarchand, *Combat*, 4 March 1949

The man condemned to death lives in the prison world where values are inverted, where the society's curse is claimed as an honour in order that it can be borne; here, the murderer, the prisoner awaiting death, is the hero, God, the Example.

Thierry Maulnier, *La Bataille*, 3 March 1949

He gilds the forces that move them with the same great, mystical, fatal passion [as Racine]. . . . [The play] is difficult to stage since, like a tragedy, it demands stylized, even mechanical, poses of which only great actors are capable.

Marc Beigbeder, *Parisien Libéré*, 10 March 1949

In reality the atmosphere of Genet's prison is remarkably like that of a big-city American high school, with its football and baseball heroes, secret societies, crushes, jealousies, favouritism, and interracial tension.

Mary McCarthy, *Partisan Review*, XXVI, No. 1 (Winter 1959)

[The play has generally been adjudged to have a more pernicious effect on audiences than this implies; but opinions are divided.]

With Genet's work we are faced with provocation, almost an attempted murder.

François Mauriac, *Figaro littéraire*, 26 March 1949

The spectacle of this fall which is transformed almost geometrically by a trick of symmetry into an ascension, disconcerts right-thinking people and upsets the sensitive.

Robert Kemp, *Le Monde français*, XIV, No. 45 (June 1945)

In the author's universe nothing remains which in any way resembles a moral awareness of good and evil. . . . It is frightening to think of the resonances that this type of theatre may have for a young boy of fifteen or sixteen; it is my opinion that it is not just on older teenagers that the toxic — and essentially sexual — action may succeed in exerting an influence.

Gabriel Marcel, *Nouvelles littéraires*, 17 March 1949

There is an undercurrent of abnormality in this wild combat which leads ultimately to murder, and at times the undercurrent develops the powerful and frightening pull of an undertow. . . . [The Murderer] is of the elect; he kills under the compulsion of evil, as some great classic heroes killed under the compulsion of the immortal gods.

There is a kind of perverse greatness in the concept, as there is a kind of perverse greatness in the fall of Lucifer in *Paradise Lost*. But it is perverse, and it is appalling.

Elliot Norton, *Boston Daily Record*, 11 March 1957

Like fingernails continuously scraping back and forth on an empty blackboard, the dialogue screeches in poetic praise of the fascinating young murderer who killed with lilac blossoms in his mouth. There is a sickeningly sweet, close-to-putrid odour that becomes almost tangible in the hot-house atmosphere created by the three bodies in interminable contest.

Donnell Stoneman, *Advocate* (Los Angeles), 22 Oct. 1975

This nightmare with three faces is searing. . . . Their excruciating choking does not let us go; it beats us.

Patrick de Rosbo, *Quotidien de Paris*, 2 March 1978

The play is completely absorbed in its prison-side point of view. . . . It is this, along with Genet's obvious ability to write theatrical dialogue, which accounts for the play's failure to horrify the spectator. . . . One can think of it either as a piece of stage fantasy or as a clinical observation, but in either case something to be left in the theatre when all is over, like a hat-check. By the end of the evening, the spectator is so detached from his normal reactions that he witnesses the climax, in which a man is strangled, with exactly the same detachment as a third prisoner in the cell, who watches without stirring a muscle.

Tom F. Driver, *Christian Century*, 12 Nov. 1958

Except for its curiosity value as being Genet's first play, this piece was hardly worth doing.

W. A. Darlington, *Daily Telegraph*, 26 June 1961

[Views on the impact of the play are informed by the perceived quality of its writing and dramatic structure. Such opinions may vary over time and in the light of the treatment the playtext receives at the hands of directors.]

The erupting, tense violence of the dialogue [is stifled] by the overwrought phrasing which quickly becomes a flood sweeping along words and ideas like victims of drowning.

Francis Ambrière, *Opéra*, 9 March 1949

Though the play's harsh, individual quality is undeniable, M. Genet's view of life is not one I profess to dig. As is customary with this author, all the characters speak with one voice, that of petulant declamation, and the action is swept forward on a tide of fierce, homosexual jealousy.

Robert Muller, *Daily Mail*, 26 June 1961

A double disappointment, then. First there was the production: superfluous, artificial, failed, it proudly and gloriously misunderstood everything, breaking the text's rigour and rhythm. Then there was the text which had shrivelled, revealing its lines and caked on make-up which was falling off in great patches. . . . It was boredom which had survived.

Pierre Marcabru, *France Soir*, 18 Sept. 1970

The black magic of Genet is fragile, because it is nothing more than a totally unjustifiable, gratuitous aesthetic construction. . . . The audience cannot help but be a little irritated by the convention of an outmoded slang and the tiresome artifice of a world where murderers . . . do not have a knife, but a rose or a lilac blossom, between their teeth.

Dominique Jamet, *Journal de Dimanche*, 4-5 March 1978

Both as a drama of ideas and as a theatre piece, *Deathwatch* lacks conviction. It rises and falls in spasms rather than collecting power for a climax. And its themes, like its characters, seem imprisoned, circling around and bumping into one another again and again, as if the playwright were trying to express mystical ideas but not managing to say them better than the first time, or even differently.

Melvin Maddocks, *Christian Science Monitor*
(Eastern Edition), 7 March 1957

It is a work of extraordinary force, written in a less brilliant, more contained, cynical style than *The Maids*, but given a sparer dialogue which, in dramatic terms, it seems to me, is more effective. . . . I continue to maintain that Jean Genet's work represents one of the theatrical events of our time.

Thierry Maulnier, *La Bataille*, 3 March 1949

The characters lie, make up stories, play tricks, become exalted and as quickly discard their exaltation like a mask. But in the play the masks are words, words from a classical dialogue which is also the dialogue of a poet.

Robert Kanters, *L'Express*, 14 Sept. 1970

However, the romantic fascination with criminals and the emotional rifts of the prison world could now seem unoriginal, but the confontations are so tautly, strongly, and brilliantly embedded in the writing that it is untouched by the passing of time.

René Bernard, *L'Express*, 27 Feb.1978

Williams's [the translator's] use of language doesn't just dust down a musty, rather stilted text. The first new translation Genet has allowed for thirty years, it restores to the play a sharpness and depth of psychological perception that might easily have been missed before. . . . [His] treatment reveals this largely disregarded text, which might have been dismissed as a B feature melodrama, to be as rich and powerful as

Genet's better known works — and in some ways more relevant and rewarding.

Robin Thornber, *The Guardian*, 11 Feb.1985

[There is clearly no consensus on what sort of play *Deathwatch* is: a naturalistic examination of the condition of prisoners, a poetic incantation, a quasi-religious celebration, a masturbatory fantasy, a psychological drama, or even a thriller. Uneasy about the combination of physicality and stylization, poetry and slang, critics have given the play any number of lables in an attempt to categorize it.]

Deathwatch is not an ordinary play which has attained the highest degree of perfection possible, it is the 'theatre of the theatre'. . . . And we must not shrink from placing Genet among the greats after Racine, Baudelaire, and Proust.

Jean-Jacques Riniéri, *La Nef*, No. 52 (March 1949)

There is much hysteria, rather more in this production than is warranted, and the translation sounds madly stilted. . . . It is a bit vague as well as nasty, but it has a strong theatrical pull like an intellectual sort of Grand Guignol.

Philip Hope-Wallace, *The Guardian*, 27 June 1961

Arcady [the director] moves from crude slang to affectation with a virtuosity which disorientates the listener while conjuring up a sense of wonder and thus unearthing in Genet's writing an as yet unrecognized Pirandellian.

Yves-Marie Choupault, *Paris-Normandie*, 25 Sept. 1970

The recent Sunday night production at the Arts seemed to approach the play as a prison melodrama, and in stumping for realistic effects it violated the spirit of the play at those very places where it was being best (realistically) acted.

Charles Marowitz, *Encore*, No.33 (Sept.-Oct. 1961)

The play is betrayed by [the production]. For example, the overture of concrete music composed of clanking chains, slamming steel doors, and banging pipes introduces a prison realism which is at odds with Genet's theatrical ceremony.

Le Promeneur de la scène, *Gazette de Lausanne*, 17-18 Oct. 1970

Deathwatch offers only stifling air . . . a black mass with an officiating priest who does not even wear a pair of underpants beneath his chasuble. In reality this black mass performed amid parallel bars and scaffolding is no more than an ordinary gym session.

Philippe Sénart, *Revue des deux mondes*, Nov. 1970

Everything is organized like a deliberately blasphemous ceremony which will elevate the worst into the best and deduce a philosophy from it. The acting itself is self-conscious, devoid of all realism. We are dealing with a ritual, a ritual of crime and homosexuality served by a majestic language that owes more to poetry than naturalism.

Henri Rabine, *La Croix*, 27-28 Sept. 1970

Jean Genet is a dramatist who offers grave difficulties to a British director. It is hard for a London director to realize that Genet's imagination is as enslaved (and also as enriched) by the ritual of the Mass as it is by blasphemy, and that the contemplating of the guillotine and Devil's Island fills him with erotic pleasure, as marks of an exalted destiny. . . . It seems to me that a certain sense of perverse grandeur is absent from the production.

Harold Hobson, *Sunday Times*, 16 April 1972

The progression is engrossing, the claustrophobic grope toward an inevitable climax wholly plausible. . . . The play is scarcely attractive, since it is all abrasions; but it is compelling to watch . . . and its multiple meanings fuse rather than intrude upon each other. . . . The play can be read as near-naturalism, followed as a story is followed, even as one listens to the incantations and watches the paroxysms that push it all toward ritual.

Walter Kerr, *New York Times*, 21 Sept. 1975

The repressed violence of the prisoners should explode in frantic dreams and frenzies, but the actors, concerned with naturalness, behave as if on the screen; they mumble and half swallow their words. They try and impose a crude psychology on this harrowing song.

Colette Godard, *Le Monde*, 28 Feb.1978

Instead of emblematic acting, here we are given a heavy-handed scrawl, a comic-strip on prisons done with rare vulgarity and ugliness. . . . It is the most stupid naturalism. Genet's text, which is written with a superb lyricism, a thousand miles removed from realism, becomes a cliché spoken with a suburban accent. . . . Don't mention passion, there isn't any . . . not a whiff of sensuality, sex is beyond the pale. For those who like Genet's work, this performance is a real torture.

Gilles Sandier, *Matin de Paris*, 8 July 1980

[Mr Rees's] designer, Andrea Montag, provides a stone flooring, a scaffold equipped with *haute surveillance* searchlights, and a warder above. The dreamy reveries are accompanied by dimming of lights and the eerie repetitive little melody composed by Andrew Dickson. But I am not sure that the sharp distinction between the two moods works happily.

Nicholas de Jongh, *The Guardian*, 18 March 1985

[There remains the argument as to the thematic content of the play: psychological or philosophical, revolutionary or reactionary? On the whole, English-language critics seem to express their opinions less equivocally.]

[*Deathwatch* is] a generally static, drab, and occasionally obscure psychological drama on the workings of the criminal mind. . . . M. Genet's unwholesome subject falls flat. It lacks the necessary impact.

Louis Calta, *New York Times*, 10 Oct. 1958

It offers a penetrating glimpse into the criminal mind and also becomes something of a reverse mirror-image of civilization. . . . It is more a play of ideas than of encounter. And, as such, it has an undeniable fascination.

Mel Gussow, *New York Times*, 12 Sept. 1975

It is much better to realize that in Jean Genet one is dealing with a pathology which has particular affinities with a widely contemporary philosophy. . . . Genet's particular kind of madness highlights the features of a certain kind of existentialism, namely the kind which begins by analyzing man in terms of his brutality and terror, and ends by regarding these as the goals of authentic selfhood.

Tom F. Driver, *Christian Century*, 12 Nov. 1958

[*Deathwatch* is] a weird, compelling ritual about the hierarchy of crime exemplified by three caged, warring prisoners. . . . From the moment when you see the white-trousered convicts pacing restlessly about their cell, Mr. Dunlop's production makes the point that this is a place where the law of the jungle pertains, and he emphasizes the umbilical

Genetesque link between sex and violence, particularly in the climactic murder where strangulation releases the pent-up physical frustration.

Michael Billington, *The Guardian*, 14 April 1972

His plays show up his obsession with power and its sexual expression, and a belief that man is all masks and role-play beset by illusion. *Deathwatch* is typical in its cross-currents of realism and fantasy, but it's far narrower in its depth and range than the later theatrical work.

Nicholas de Jongh, *The Guardian*, 18 March 1985

Genet was a great image-maker but a limited thinker. He ritualizes the power element in human relationships but he does not so much advance and test his ideas as restate them in a lush, rhetorical prose. . . . In *Deathwatch* he accepts and even rejoices in the prison hierarchy (a mirror of the outside world) that means that Green Eyes retains his eminence even after a jealous cellmate has killed the young delinquent. . . . What I find stifling, even when Genet is as well performed as this, is the glorification of death and the conservative notion that all life is illusion incapable of change.

Michael Billington, *The Guardian*, 26 Oct. 1987

Although apparently realist and psychological, the play develops a dazzling, private fantasy and reaches towards the border between dream and reality. . . . The death which awaits Yeux-Verts is ambiguous: it liberates him and crowns him king in Evil, but it also casts him in advance into a role set by society. He derives his glory not from being a murderer but from being in his turn the one chosen to go under the knife. . . . At the Recamier theatre, we are told a very different story, straight from a rather unusual problem page, enlivened by some exceptional gymnastics.

Robert Abirached, *Nouvelle Revue française*, 1 Nov. 1970

[The author himself has little to say on the play and less on its message.]

You are referring to *Haute surveillance*? I've nothing to say, since I've written the play. . . . Yes, it was written at the same time as *Les Bonnes*. . . . Yes, there are parallels between the two plays: I've simply changed cells. From Madame's bedroom to the prison. My work rotates around the same problem. In the play I'm finishing at the moment, it will be the same thing. There's only ever one problem to resolve.

Genet, to Henri Spade, *Paris-Presse*, 24 Feb. 1949

How intensely we wish that every prison and every cell were to be in reality like the theatrical image we present to you of them.

Genet, cited in a programme note,
Théâtre des Mathurins, 26 Feb. 1949.

I would like this play to be put at the back of the fourth volume of my complete works, like a footnote or a rough copy of a play. And since I'm expressing wishes, I would also like it never to be performed again.

It's difficult for me to remember when and in what circumstances I wrote it. Probably out of boredom, or it slipped out. That will be it, it escaped from me.

Genet, in a note dated Sept. 1967,
in Oeuvres complètes, Vol IV (Paris: Gallimard, 1968)

The Maids (Les Bonnes)

Written: begun in 1946, under title *La Tragédie des confidentes*. A three- or four-act version was shown to Jouvet in July 1946; many revisions between Oct. 1946 and April 1947.

First production: Théâtre de l'Athénée, Paris, 19 April 1947 (dir. Louis Jouvet).

First British production: in French, Royal Court Theatre, London, 11 Nov. 1952 (dir. Peter Zadek).

First American production: Tempo Playhouse, New York, 6 May 1955 (dir. Strowan Robertson).

Major revivals: Théâtre de la Huchette, Paris, 13 Jan. 1954 (dir. Tania Balachova); New Lindsay Theatre, London, 5 June 1956 (dir. Peter Zadek); Odéon-Théâtre de France, Paris, 18 May 1963 (dir. Jean-Marie Serreau); Théâtre Montparnasse, Paris, 27 June 1963 (dir. Jean-Marie Serreau, all black cast); Aldana Theatre, New York, 14 Nov. 1963 (dir. Aldo Bruzzicholli); Oxford Playhouse, Oxford, 3 March 1964 (dir. Minos Volanakis); La Mama Experimental Theatre Club, New York, Oct. 1964 (dir. Tom O'Horgan); Forum Theatre, Berlin, 26 Feb. 1965 (Living Theatre on tour, dir. Judith Malina, all-male cast); Teatro Poliorama, Barcelona, 21 Feb. 1969, and widely on tour (dir. Victor Garcia); Comédie de St. Etienne, St. Etienne, 2 March 1971 (dir. Roland Monod, mixed cast); Espace Pierre Cardin, Paris, 13 March 1971 (dir. Victor Garcia); Théâtre de la Cité Internationale, Paris, 20 April 1971 (dir. Jean-Marie Patte, all-male cast); Young Vic, London, 13 April 1972 (dir. Frank Dunlop, with *Deathwatch*); Greenwich Theatre, London, 14 Feb. 1974 (dir. Minos Volanakis); Palace Théâtre, Paris, 10 March 1977 (dir. Henri Ronse); Lyric Studio, Hammersmith, 13 Oct. 1981 (dir. Clare Davidson); The Pit, Barbican, London 12 Oct. 1987 (dir. Gerard Murphy with Ultz).

First published: in the review *L'Arbalète,* No 12 (May 1947), p. 47-92; a second version which followed Jouvet's production appeared with the original published version in *Les Bonnes,* Sceaux: Jean-Jacques Pauvert, 1954; later editions follow the Jouvet text with minor textual variants especially in stage directions.

Translations: as *The Maids,* Bernard Frechtman, following 1947 text, New York: Grove Press, 1954, and London: Faber, 1957; David Rudkin, 1987, for Royal Shakespeare Company, following 1968 *Oeuvres complètes* text, unpublished.

Enclosed in their mistress's bedroom, two maids, the sisters Claire and Solange, perform a nightly ceremony in which they act out the complex relationships of dominance and subjugation which pertain between themselves, and between themselves and their mistress. The ceremony's climax is to be the symbolic murder of their mistress. It advances unevenly: the vindictive expression of their mutual loathing and inadequacy bursts through their excited recitation of their litany of revolt. The climax is forestalled, amid recriminations, by the imminent return of the hated mistress. But this time it is to be different. Unusually exalted, and fearful of being discovered as the authors of letters incriminating their mistress's lover, they resolve to finish the ceremony by poisoning the mistress herself. This plan is frustrated by the premature departure of the mistress following her discovery of her lover's unexpected release from prison. The maids are once more thrown back on themselves. They begin the ceremony again, but more frenetically. Claire as the mistress intones the loathsomeness of servants; as she tires, Solange launches into an impassioned monologue in which she sees herself as the beatified murderer at the head of a triumphant parade of dignitaries and serving people. It is Claire, though, who calmly initiates the final act by ordering her sister to serve her the poisoned tea. Solange is left to proclaim their freedom from servanthood.

[Although *The Maids* was Genet's second play, Jouvet's production was the first opportunity for drama critics to evaluate Genet the dramatist.

Their responses anticipate the controversy which will continue to surround his plays. Whether attacking or defending, their vocabulary is rarely neutral.]

The play's style is so inconceivably overblown, . . . it is twaddle or, better still, amphigory, the linguistic hotchpotch from the Saint Ouen fair at the time of the King's Troupe who alone were allowed to use reasoned speech. . . . Here we wander from incoherence to non-sensical rambling, from antilogy to logomachia. . . . It is a work whose pretentiousness hides a vacuum, just as a golden sheet hides a nag.

Hervé Lauwick, *Noir et Blanc*, 7 May 1947

This disconcerting and masochistic text can only be taken for an inconsequential entertainment lacking all literary pretensions.

Georges Huisman, *La France au combat*, 24 April 1947

The Maids is an interminable work in which monumental pretentiousness is trying desperately to have itself taken seriously. The challenge to morality and society is somewhat puerile and is never really worrying.

B. de Garambé, *Rivarol*, 21 Jan. 1954

The plot is accompanied by jets of words, blasts of images, and garlands of paradoxes; the brilliant and careful construction painstakingly creates an unbreathable atmosphere. . . . The essence of theatre is here: the fusion of text, direction, and acting.

Pierre Lagarde, *Libération*, 20 April 1947

This play is a black jewel which is given all its brilliance by the spare rigour of Ms. Balachova's production. What will never be forgiven Jean Genet is that he has suddenly given demons a burning voice which is more than human; he has given them sumptuous words and images which only those who have been without a voice for so long can discover. The subject of the play is the action and the thoughts of confidants when they leave the stage after having patiently listened to the tragic hero talk of his loves and exploits.

Jacques Lemarchand, *Figaro littéraire*, 23 Jan. 1954

It crackles with satanic fury as the flame of the drama rises. A more experienced playwright might have made it a perfect specimen of construction, an exercise in suspense technique, but conventional technique is of little use to Genet. Its dialogue is often repetitious and the squeamish may take offence at its brazen language, but Genet gives here to an ignoble tale a touch of genuine tragedy.

Thomas Quinn Curtiss, *New York Herald Tribune*, 18 Jan. 1954

[At the first production a short Giraudoux play was the balm used to soothe a disturbed public. Comfort has never been part of Genet's theatrical credo.]

M. Jean Genet imposes on us a clinical document of barely tolerable harshness and cynicism. Jean Giraudoux offers an entertainment full of casual irony. The former irritates and disturbs us and the latter calms and reassures us.

Guy Joly, *L'Aurore*, 24 April 1947

To see it is like watching an adhesive bandage being repeatedly torn off an unhealed wound.

Kenneth Tynan, *Evening Standard*, 14 Nov. 1952

The evening makes Strindberg's *Miss Julie* look like a Sunday school outing.

Philip Hope-Wallace, *Manchester Guardian*, 13 Nov. 1952

I hated *The Maids*. I still do because it is not true to life and it drags our minds constantly through the slimy depths of two unreal and fabricated souls. . . . On leaving the theatre you feel ugly, ashamed of yourself. Ashamed to belong to the human species. You have to be sadistic to take pleasure in such a spectacle.

Robert Kemp, *Le Monde*, 15 Jan. 1954

[As Genet's most often performed play, *The Maids* has been exposed to a variety of directorial approaches to which critics have had the opportunity to apply historical perspective. Again there is division: for some the passage of time has enhanced the effect of the play whereas for others it has exposed its inherent weaknesses.]

What an utter disappointment. What seven years ago had seemed something exceptional, rare, now seems unbelievable, adolescent, and disarmingly conventional. Behind each line, you sense the author's devilish desire to provoke, shock, outrage the audience. . . . Everything rings false. The maids talk like philosophers and the mistress like a charlady. . . . The badly balanced scenes are interminable and the whole thing exudes a deadly boredom.

André Ransan, *L'Aurore*, 15 Jan. 1954

When the American premiere of *The Maids* was held one evening . . . in Manhattan over 20 years ago everything about the play seemed startling. Closet doors were opening, and the repressions, hostilities, and trappings of the guilt cult were paraded on stage for substantial impact. Today these once provocative melodies are almost yawn-inspiring, and the ploy of casting males in the female roles comes across more as a gimmick than anything else.

J. Moriarty, *Advocate* (Los Angeles), 16 Jan. 1974

Why do Jean Genet's ferocious images of power, sex, and death seem nowadays so tawdry and camp? . . . Fantasies of power and vengeance, Genet suggests, are the most we can expect of a society based on the horrible machismo of authority: all our relationships are primarily erotic, and society is, therefore, merely a collective enactment of deep and instinctual sexual games, the acceptable, public way for us to justify our own private and humiliating longings. . . . But fantasy — however acute — is an exceptionally limited form. To be trapped within the skull of the fantasist is to be denied the essential dialogue of art — the dialogue between an inner self and an exterior world. A real-life revolution breaks in on the voyeurisitic make-believe of *The Balcony*, but in *Deathwatch* and *The Maids* there is no such perspective, no recognizable distance on the spiral of obsession. . . . The production, by Gerard Murphy and the designer Ultz, captures brilliantly the mood of sexual threnody which underpins Genet's work. But it cannot disguise a basic deforming monotony. Genet states a theme but cannot develop an argument.

Andrew Rissick, *The Independent*, 26 Oct. 1987

Beneath the asocial protest and sexual fantasies another discovery has been made: a supremely theatrical and poetic, awesome illustration of the layers of sham and pretence to which human relationships are reduced. The sordid little story has become the poisoned tragedy of humanity condemned to pure appearance and total irreality, completely lacking in identity and order.

Bertrand Poirot-Delpech, *Le Monde*, 20 May 1961

Have Genet's successive works since that date made it easier for us to understand his intentions and made his ritual more familiar to us? It is very apparent that *The Maids* has more chance of reaching an appraised public today. Its violence is no longer shocking and what is now glacially and purely communicated to us is a tragedy on the spell of hatred, with its inexorable outcome.

Gilbert Guilleminault, *L'Aurore*, 4 Sept. 1963

We are probably more moved today than 23 years ago by this incredible ceremony. It is a tragi-comedy played out by two women trapped in their condition as servants but it reaches the pitch of delirium expressed in sumptuous, baroque tirades where each word has its place, where each image stays brilliant through its very extremeness.

Guy Dumur, *Nouvel Observateur*, 22 March 1971

Once stripped of its flowery setting and returned to its raw state, the play was aggressive and fascinating. By creating a provocative, liturgical ceremonial, Garcia had gone beyond playing with life and death: alienated to the point of identification, Claire sacrifices herself in Madame's place and thus gives a 'true image born of a false spectacle'. . . . Genet's play, and all his theatre, perhaps need today to be extended by this indefinable 'something extra' which the author himself recognized in the Spanish production.

Lucien Attoun, *Quinzaine littéraire*, 1 April 1971

The Maids presents two clear alternatives: either a naturalistic bedroom, where two girls play out their ritual in defiance of their surroundings; or a ritualistic space . . . where periodic slumps into normal behaviour clash with the surroundings.

In her set for Greenwich, Yolande Sonnabend has tried to combine these alternatives in a single image. . . . It is an appealing idea, and it fails to work; it also shows how far we have travelled since Genet made his first impact on our club theatre stages in the 'fifties. He is now a classic. The basic idea, of two wretched girls escaping into criminally glamorous fantasy when their mistress is out of the house, has lost its impact. So we move into the phase of baroque production, with emphasis on overblown decor and on the rhetoric of Genet's inverted theology, rather than on the clear dramatic situation and feeling for character on which the work rests.

Irving Wardle, *The Times*, 27 Feb. 1974

[Not surprisingly the play has been interpreted from a wide range of perspectives: notably, clinical psychology, social psychology, sociology, existentialism, and aesthetics.]

The slovenliness of its tone, the vulgarity of its characters, spoil the skilful treatment of its subject matter and its well observed psychological situations which could have been moving. Unfortunately, hysteria does not work on the stage. Genet makes intriguing use of the automaton-like behaviour of the mentally unstable and of an interesting example of identification. The maids cannot free themselves from the authority of their mistress. They have made a transfer: the Mistress becomes the Mother, she issues orders, . . . the Master becomes the Father. The Oedipus complex is here represented as the basis of jealousy. It is necessary to kill the Mistress in order to free themselves from her. It is impossible to leave: a psychological enslavement cannot be broken. If he had not given in to the temptation to create scandal, M. Genet could have given us a harrowing account of domestic psychology.

Henriette Brunot, *Psyché: Revue internationale de psychanalyse et des sciences humaines*, June 1974

Certainly the play is not without interest. It is the account of a psychopathic case which is aggravated by the role of servant. In this mixture simmer complexes and repression, but what dominates is the will of the two servants to break out at whatever cost from their pitiable condition. The stifling atmosphere of this drama of paranoia is intensified by the size of the stage, the scruffiness of the set, and the slowness of the production.

J. Guignebert, *Libération*, 15 Jan. 1954

The play is revitalized as an exploration of the condition of the servant, of its incessant and intolerable contradictions: extremes of 'luxury and filth', sainthood and criminality. . . . It is also . . . an exploration (as Sartre long ago pointed out, as Lacan would have recognized, and as the general existential-psychoanalytical emphasis of the production makes abundantly clear) of every shade — overt and implicit transexuality being the most obvious — of 'deviant' sexuality; of what it is like to desire above everything else to be something you cannot be.

Alan Jenkins, *Times Literary Supplement*, 30 Oct. 1981

This savage and claustral dramatic poem is one of the most impressive of contemporary works for the theatre. . . . Ostensibly, the terms of *The Maids* are those of class antagonism; ultimately, it is concerned with the mystery of identity.

Richard Hayes, *Commonweal*, 22 July 1955

A social position is always a mask which the powerful find easy to assume but which is deadly for the weak who wish to imitate the powerful.

Michel Zéraffa, *Europe*, July-Aug. 1961

According to Genet, true reality can only be apprehended through a ceremonial of lies and deceptions which in its turn loses power if it doesn't lead to the purity of death.

Robert Abirached, *Etudes*, July-Aug. 1961

It is not a sociological play on cleaners and servants. It is an example of the theatre of cruelty and the psychological slaughter through which an individual tries to become whole again, tries to repossess him/herself through the destruction of the other.

P.C., *Rouge*, 14 May 1976

But despite line-by-line forcefulness and the creation of sustained tension in the longer passages, there was none of the involvement between the characters that differentiates theatre from recitation. . . . For all its psychological overtones, the play is basically a social tract.

Richard F. Shepard, *New York Times*, 15 Nov. 1963

Yet another bitter, violent, existential theme of social despair and moral disgust which loses its way amid a mass of tiresome declamation and a certain outrageousness of tone which does shock on occasions.

Surcouf, *Semaine de Paris*, 30 April 1947

The 'decadent' French drama to-day is explosive. Heavy with guilt, resentment, self-loathing, yearning for deliverance through destruction, self-immolation, expiation, sacrifice or heroic affirmation, it is an expression of the martyrdom of the French middle-class conscience after the degradation of Munich, the shame of defeat, the conflict between collaborator and resistant, the terrible dichotomy — coupled with impotence — that tears away at the country's vitals to this day.

Harold Clurman, *New Republic*, 23 Aug. 1948

The Maids is more an evocation of the Hegelian dialectic of the master and slave relationship than the Marxist dialectic of class struggle in that the same drama could unfurl on all other levels: the lover and the loved, the occupier and the occupied — in short, wherever the oppression of man by man is possible.

Jeanne Delhomme, *Le Cheval de Troie*, Aug.-Sept. 1947

Genet likes metaphor. He indicates the possibilities of crossing from one reality to another without wishing there to be an end. The knot is untied before ever being tied. . . . His metaphors are more important than the subject matter, which serves only as a pretext for creating shimmering reflections. . . . I think that the critics have not spoken sufficiently of Genet's language, rather they have produced article after article on anecdotal material and the emotional life of the homosexual thief.

Adrien Gentil, *Lettres nouvelles*, 5 May 1954

[When the critics take up Gentil's challenge to comment on style and dramatic technique, the result is once more conflict. Those in the naturalist tradition object to a self-indulgent artificiality in the writing; others sense a move into a poetic and ritual form.]

However little Genet wanted to give in to theatrical necessity, he could not completely do away with speech. All poetry disappeared through this breach in the impressive style of his novels. Credibility went with it. There remains a certain unease and boredom which increases until the flat, fabricated denouement. Genet has chosen to be in revolt, to defend ideas which he alone has. It is not at all surprising then that he fails when he tries to have someone else say words which he alone can articulate.

Arts, 21 Jan. 1954

We are held by the grip of that central, tragic dramatic process which Aristotle called the agon; that process which goes on, gets more and more completely and openly ritualized (as it must do), for the final stages whereby a murderer is transfigured into society's victim are still too strong a taboo to be surrounded by any but the most awesome magic. . . . What Genet gives us is an utterly dark agon with no release for, instead of plumbing the irrational and bringing back light, he stops short at its margin where he gives us invocation, gesture, and rhetoric, platonic essences of evil.

Martin Shuttleworth, *The Listener*, 13 June 1963

The genius of Genet is that he is constantly whipping one mask off the next, in an endless succession of changes, but ultimately, no matter how many disguises are donned and doffed, there must be a face somewhere behind it all. For clearly the only way to judge illusions is by referring them to the reality which evoked them. That *The Maids* never does, and so we are left with the gutsy evocation of style unhinged from content.

Charles Marowitz, *Plays and Players*, April 1974

Unfortunately, the tone adopted is such as to make you immediately adopt a defensive attitude towards the author and his characters. I cannot remember having heard in the theatre more uncompromisingly false and pretentious language. Moreover, you sense that the author wishes to provoke the audience and push it to the edge of its patience. The right response would surely be not to be taken in, to maintain a disdainful and indifferent attitude. I have to admit that I found that impossible to do.

Gabriel Marcel, *Revue des hommes et mondes*, July 1947

Such a subject could lend itself to a virulent social satire or to a macabre, humorous riddle. In actual fact, Jean Genet's dialogue is spoilt by the most disappointing literary attitudinizing; his maids have evidently been fed the same platitudes as the characters in his novels. . . . How could a play cross the footlights when the atmosphere on stage is so false from beginning to end?

René Lalou, *Gavroche*, 1 May 1947

It would be the greatest of errors to see the play as realist. Genet's violence is of a different order: the informed rigour of his art, his control of a luxuriant language, respect the spectator. Here we are dealing with theatre as initiation, theatre reassuming all its powers as a savage rite. . . . Genet's genius has rediscovered the only possible route for poetic theatre: the mythical reconstruction of a universe from an extreme situation.

Jean-Jacques Riniéri, *La Nef*, May 1947

The difficulty in doing this play is that while it appears to be a realistic piece about two servants suffering from a consuming envy of their depraved and wealthy mistress . . . it is actually a poetic drama of a kind that our audiences would immediately label 'morbid'.

Harold Clurman, *New Republic*, 23 Aug. 1948

The maids speak like queens in a tragedy, that is to say completely artificially. But the ritual sacrifice that they act out to its final moment . . . elevates them, inspires them. The spoken word becomes white-hot, as Artaud wished it to be. They take us into the realm of poetic trance where the wind of true drama blows.

Georges Lerminier, *Gazette de Lausanne*, 17 May 1961

We are a long way from social satire and just as far from psychological drama. Genet's language . . . does not allow such interpretations. His language is that of tragedy. Apart from the scenes with the mistress, there is nothing which makes us think of the ordinariness of the characters you find in realist theatre.

Guy Dumur, Théâtre populaire, Jan.-Feb. 1954

Now freed from the anecdotal and parodic, *The Maids* appears in all its force as frenzied parable, as a glorification of Evil, pushed to sacrifice, a stunning black mass which is raised to the level of sacrilege and despair. It is no longer a play, it is a rite in which is expressed (with a symbolic, clear cruelty) the weight of a selfish society which condemns its oppressed to crime.

Matthieu Galey, Combat, 9 April 1970

The Nuria Espert company's production has respected the text's subversive and, at times, sacrilegious violence. . . . Madame's apartment is devoid of all realism, more like a ritual space. The matt metal mirrors and the round bed draped in black silk seem to be the accessories for a sacrifice. The two leading actresses, Nuria Espert and Julieta Serrano, impart trance-like rhythm and tension to the magic they weave. Whether they are atop the strange cothorni with bells in which they ape their mistress's mortal superiority or whether they are dragging themselves around the floor like deranged creatures, the extreme frenzy of their acting and their diction is striking. Laid bare and heightened in this way, the play is revealed to be one of the few modern — yet classical — tragedies. We are a long way from the chic which Bérard had created for Jouvet, and the light entertainment given to us by Yvette Etiévant and Monique Mélinard. Clearly Garcia is right, and Genet recognized this recently when he described the production as an admirable version which renews his text and gives it new dimensions.

Bertrand Poirot-Delpech, Le Monde, 9 April 1970

Victor Garcia . . . memorably treated the play as a perverted, erotic religious ritual. With Minos Volanakis's Greenwich production, however, we return abruptly to square one: a cold, temperate story of two maids and their mistress conducted with all the blazing passion of afternoon in the Pump Rooms at Bath.

It is impossible to ignore the fact that the play is, in Sartre's words, a Black Mass. . . . Admittedly the play is also full of political, sexual, and social reverberations about the constant division of mankind into who and whom, the dominator and the dominated; but through it all runs the notion that the two oppressed maids are conducting an obscene religious ritual in an elegant Louis Quinze bedroom. . . . Without the strong pulse of religious ritual and liturgical savagery, the play seems a small-scale affair.

Michael Billington, *The Guardian*, 20 Feb. 1974

In Genet's universe, murder is all at once an act of aesthetic beauty, sexual excitement, and spiritual transcendance; and it is fitting that it should be accompanied here by the sound of the mass. . . . Both the production and the translation bring out the element of religious ritual that informs the play.

Michael Billington, *The Guardian*, 26 Oct. 1987

[Experimentation with the play has not only taken the form of changing settings and directorial approaches, but has also extended to casting. Following the author's suggestion, productions have used male as well as female performers, not without danger.]

If I had to put on a play where women would have a part, I would demand that the roles were taken by young boys and I would warn the public of this by a large notice nailed to the right or left of the set throughout the whole performance.

Genet, *Our Lady of the Flowers*,
trans. Bernard Frechtman (London: Blond, 1964)

More is involved here than simply introducing another level of reality, for if the audience can believe that the actors are really transvestites who are using this theatre and this audience to achieve a status that society denies them, then both theatrical conventions and the security of the audience will be profoundly disturbed. . . . Somewhere, however, we must catch glimpses of the real agony of the unfulfilled transvestites. . . . We should have seen transvestites transforming whatever they use into ritualistic devices, not actors asking us to suspend our disbelief in makeshift props. . . . We must see the properties being transformed in order to understand the ritual aspect of the play. . . . Unfortunately, the lack of a clear directorial viewpoint made the evening a camp instead of an illumination.

Sidney S. Walter, *Village Voice*, 29 Oct. 1964

Faced with these three men in drag (men and not youths) the audience, once the initial shock of transvestism was over . . . and as the transvestites became more and more identified — and this was the mistake — with their female characters, the audience soon found itself in the presence of three women. . . . With this we were back with illusion; the disjuncture was abolished. . . . In order that the 'tourniquet' should work, the adolescents acting the parts must clearly remain adolescents speaking out on stage. . . . Only 'a sign charged with signs, a simple metaphor for what he is to represent'. Only then does theatre become once more the locus of absolute revolt which hits at one and the same time a society and one of its most crude rites: the theatre as it is usually played.

Gilles Sandier, *Théâtre et Combat* (Paris: Stock, 1970)

The prison without walls that Claire and Solange construct for themselves has so little to do with sexual difference that transvestism at first looks like a travesty or an irrelevance. But when drag effects are so exquisitely controlled as they are here, the new level of meaning added to the play is entirely in the spirit of Genet. A man plays a woman playing a maid playing a female employer playing a dutiful wife. . . . Impersonation is all; when we desist from it we die. Small wonder that an average theatregoer should, in his mind's eye, reach for the bottle and retire between the sheets.

Malcolm Bowie, *Times Literary Supplement*, 13 Nov. 1987

[To a large extent the critics' interpretations have followed directorial leads over the years, starting with realism in 1947.]

To place it as a play, maybe it would be sufficient to recall that it nearly had the title *The Tragedy of the Confidantes*. In this case, it is about the problems and behaviour of the young. Jean Genet is a dramatic writer. It's something that I've rarely seen in a young author. His style is exact, concise, direct. . . . This play belongs to no genre. Nevertheless, it seems to me to be political or social in keeping with current thinking.

Louis Jouvet, to J.-B. Jeener, *Figaro*, 16 April 1947

What attracted me to Genet was not his poetry but more his images and actions. . . . I tried to question my own frame of mind and how I see things. I took the text as an outline and scenario to be developed. . . . The scenic space is an open space, a sort of operating room, a ceremonial space in which to study characters. . . . Above all I tried to restrict as far as I could all possible diversions into literary, poetic, or anecdotal themes. I worked theatrically; my work concerned actions, movement, not ideas.

Victor Garcia, to Jean-Jacques Olivier, *Combat*, 3 March 1971

[Genet himself has voiced his own opposition to realistic treatment of his text on several occasions.]

Commissioned by an actor who was once famous, my play was written out of vanity, but also boredom. All the same — and I'm still talking of its composition — I had already been disturbed by the dull sadness of a form of theatre which was too exact a reflection of the visible world, of man's and not God's actions, and so I tried to achieve a disjunction which, while still allowing a declamatory tone, would turn theatre back on itself. I was hoping to bring about the abolition of characters — which usually persist because of the psychological tradition — to replace them by signs which are as far removed as possible from what they are supposed to represent, but yet still connected to them. It was through this sole link that I was hoping to unite the author with the audience. In short, I was hoping to have the characters on stage be nothing other than the metaphors of what they were supposed to represent.

Genet, 'Lettre à Pauvert', in *Les Bonnes*
(Sceaux: Jean-Jacques Pauvert, 1954)

It's a tale, that is to say a form of allegory whose first intention, when I was writing it, was to disgust myself by showing or refusing to show who I was, and the second was to create a certain unease in the auditorium. . . .

It must be believable and unbelievable at the same time, but in order to be believable the actresses must not act in a realistic way. . . .

One thing must be written: the play is not a defence of the serving condition. I presume there is a union for servants — that is not our concern.

Genet, 'Comment jouer *Les Bonnes*',
in *Les Bonnes* (Décines: L'Arbalète, 1963)

The Balcony (Le Balcon)

Written: 1954-55.
First production: in English, Arts Theatre Club, London, 22 April 1957 (dir. Peter Zadek).
First American production: Circle in the Square, 28 Feb. 1960 (dir. José Quintero).
First French production: Théâtre de la Gymnase, 18 May 1960 (dir. Peter Brook).

Major revivals: Théâtre des Nations, Paris, 6 July 1961 (dir. Leon Epp); Actor's Workshop, San Francisco, 29 March 1963 (dir. Herbert Blau); Oxford Playhouse, Oxford, 28 Feb. 1967 (dir. Minos Volanakis); Théâtre du Gymnase, Marseille, 21 Nov. 1969 (dir. Antoine Bourseiller); Ruth Escobar Theatre, Sao Paolo, 27 Dec. 1969 (dir. Victor Garcia); Théâtre National de Strasbourg, 20 Jan. 1971 (dir. André Steiger); Aldwych Theatre, London, 25 Nov. 1971 (dir. Terry Hands); Théâtre Recamier, Paris, 22 Jan. 1975 (dir. Antoine Bourseiller); Piccolo Teatro, Milan, Dec. 1976 (dir. Giorgio Strehler); Performing Garage, New York, 17 Nov. 1979 (dir. Richard Schechner); Comédie Française, Paris, 14 Dec. 1985 (dir. Georges Levaudant); Barbican Theatre, London, 9 July 1987 (dir. Terry Hands).

First published: in 15 scenes in two acts, Décines: L'Arbalète, 1956; a second version, in nine scenes with a preceding note from the author, Décines: L'Arbalète, 1960; a third version, in nine scenes, with 'Comment jouer *Le Balcon*', Décines: L'Arbalète, 1962;. this text, with minor revisions, reprinted in *Oeuvres complètes*, Vol. IV (Paris: Gallimard, 1986).

Translations: by Bernard Frechtman, version in nine scenes with variants, New York: Grove and London: Faber, 1957; revised version following 1962 text, London: Faber, 1965; by Terry Hands and Barbara Wright, 15-scene version, with extended revolutionary scene and respecting revised version of final scene, 1971, unpublished; by Robert David MacDonald, with reduced revolutionary scene, 1982, unpublished.

The play opens with Irma, the madame of the house of illusions, supervising the set of one of her client's erotic enactments. The Bishop, the Judge, the General, and the Tramp are regular customers who come to play out, and seek fulfilment in, scenes of submission and domination. Their fantasy world is fragile, for all the pomp of their costumes and their rhetorical flourishes on the nature of role, function, and being. They are anxious lest anything interrupt their fantasies — a detail forgotten, a door opened, a scream from another cubicle; they become increasingly nervous about the progress of a rebellion, which is ever present in the rattling of gun-fire, and about the ineffectiveness of the Chief of Police to control the political situation and protect them. Away from the sets, Irma exists in a world where profit and takings are calculated, but it is only slightly more sure and equally marked by frustration and unfulfilled desires. The rebellion is as threatening to her as it is to her clients. Her businesslike severity is exposed as a veneer as she seeks an impossible intimacy with Carmen, her favoured employee, who dreams of returning to the fantasies of the clients. Arthur, the pimp, is similarly a creature of the house who stalks its sets and corridors, frightened of the street. George, the Chief of Police, offers scant comfort and protection: his view of the rebellion as a form of play-acting fails to convince Irma, who fears the real passion of the rebels, inspired by Chantal, a former employee. George is more intent on seeking immortality as one of the figures of the house of illusions, but his desire is frustrated as no client has yet asked for his role. The uneasy peace is shattered by a shot that kills Arthur. It is questioned by the arrival of the Envoy, a real dignitary. The pure irreality of illusion is sullied by contact with political reality. In the camp of the rebels a similar struggle between authenticity and emblem is being waged. Roger's love for Chantal is thwarted by the demands of the rebels for a figure to lead their attack on the royal palace. Feeling is subjugated to a battle of allegories. Meanwhile the Envoy is organizing resistance: Irma is to replace the invisible Queen. Surrounded by her Bishop, Judge, General, and Tramp, she appears on the Balcony. It is these images that triumph as Chantal is shot as she comes onto the balcony. Once having assumed a public presence, the figures plot to retain their power by swopping ornament for responsibility. They will remain safe from the anger of the Chief of Police until he too is immortalized in the house of illusions. This happens when Roger returns to the brothel to enact the role of the Hero, the Chief of Police. In a desperate attempt to usurp the power of the Hero, Roger castrates himself. The Chief of Police, intact, proceeds triumphantly to his mausoleum. It remains for Irma to extinguish the lights of her house of illusions, sending everyone home, including the audience, now identified with the clients and failed revolutionaries.

[Unequivocal praise for this play is scant. By-now customary charges of obscurantism, sensationalism, and puerility are more prevalent.]

A requiem for human illusions, *The Balcony* has a funereal greatness, a destructive passion, a rabid desire for annihilation, all of which make it a devastating, cataclysmic work whose bitter, desperate, sarcastic, and revolutionary poetic power has no equal in contemporary theatre.

Pierre Marcabru, *Arts*, 25 May 1960

Though many people would find *The Balcony* a pretty nauseous stew, it is neither without pungent wit nor fantasy of a macabre kind. . . . The ideas of contrasting and superimposing private and public fantasies of power make a sizeable gesture to the new theatre of Grand Guignol and will be seized on in some quarters as deeply significant, which it is not. Nor is it very good theatre, though the scenes of agonized erotic make-believe are well written, ingeniously thought out, and by no means dull.

Philip Hope-Wallace, *Manchester Guardian*, 24 April 1957

The play is a cryptogram and I very seriously and very deeply fear for the future of a theatre which goes down the road of pretentious obscurantism. For the real public, the public at large, once having got over their initial astonishment, will be quick to abandon the temples where they celebrate such impenetrable services. . . . [*The Balcony* forms part of modern dramatists'] preposterous monument to the glory of confusion, pathos, false poetry, sexual obsession, and filth, and above all to a total inability of authors to express whatever ideas they have with clarity.

Jean-Jacques Gautier, *Figaro*, 24 May 1960

[*The Balcony* is] a philosophic farce, full of repetitions, stagnant and monotonous passages shot through with the power of obscene and sumptuous language and a baroque and poetic mind. . . . There is as well so much incoherence, commotion, turgidity that a good number of bored spectators angered by this 'twisting of being around the void' finally began to whistle.

Paul Gordeaux, *France Soir*, 20 May 1960

He peppers his involved argument with blasphemy and salts it with rudery. But the evening which begins by being outrageous ends by being quite suffocatingly dull.

Alan Dent, *News Chronicle*, 23 April 1957

What appalled me about this stark evening was that so much brilliance should have gone into so much brutal writing. The play is a sinister kind of *Alice in Wonderland*, combining imagination and finesse with the sniggering smut of a small boy.

Cecil Wilson, *Daily Mail*, 23 April 1957

All thoughts about Genet lead back to the same point. His masquerades, his acts of violence are the ever recurring dream of the small boy acting the character he wants to grow up to be.

Georges Portal, *Ecrits de Paris*, Sept. 1960

[*The Balcony*] satisfies to a degree hitherto unknown our contemporary dramatic appetite for violence, perversion, and squalour. . . . It is evident, from particular remarks of the characters and from the general tone of the play, that M. Genet designed the bawdy-house masquerades as a bitter commentary on daylight society. . . . Doubtless there is a great deal of hypocrisy and falsity in our civilization, but the author seems ill-equipped to point it out. To consult him on such matters is very much like turning to the Marquis de Sade for knowledge of the common life and the social utility of medieval castles. That is to say, M. Genet's vision of society is both perverse and private, and his play is a species of Grand Guignol — arresting, horrific, and trivial.

David Malcolm, *New Yorker*, 12 March 1960

[In an attempt to work out the meaning, one New York critic invited the comments of three psychoanalysts following a performance, and such psychological interpretation has continued to be a favoured route through which to approach the play.]

[For Harold Greenwald, *The Balcony* presents] 'an acting out of infantile fantasies of sexuality in a brothel. . . . Genet demonstrates infantile sexual acting-out to be a disguised force in the psychology of authority in everyday political life.' J. L. Moreno compared it to a dreamer, a profound psychotic hallucination of revolt against everything in society that stinks. [Benjamin Nelson observed]: 'We cannot achieve meaning unless we assume roles and thus recognize authentication. But through these very roles we strive for existence, for life, while at the same time we die.'

Edwin Fancher, *Village Voice*, 22 Dec. 1960

Life is unbearable if looked straight in the face, truth is cruel, therefore you have to lie to others and to yourself. But lying is not just a defence, it is also an attempt to dominate, to take over a world that denies its own existence. . . . Throughout the whole play, we see illusion growing until it has the force of reality and, in a parallel movement, this reality breaks up into multiple illusions. . . . Man is no more than a cipher in a void or at least an absurd dream in an absurd universe.

Jacques Bauchère, *Confluent* (Rabat), Sept. 1960

In Genet's vision man fears both life and death; and therefore spends his time stage-managing a persona which defends him from the threats of the present and negotiates his idea of glory in the future. *The Balcony* is a brilliant attempt to incarnate this yearning for heroism and symbolic immortality. . . . Genet's play is about the power of imagery, and the desire of man to plant the idea of himself in others. . . . This is the psychic capitalism we call celebrity. . . . In the clutter of Terry Hands's expensive production, the important ideas in Genet's play go unfocused. Sense gives way to spectacle. Instead of illuminating the mind, the stage pictures weary it. The greatest illusion of an evening that mythologizes illusions is that we have been enthralled.

John Lahr, *Vogue*, Nov. 1987

[*The Balcony* treats] Genet's favourite, obsessive theme: living is to go from being to seeming, to embracing a myth, playing a role. Human destiny is not played out between dream and reality, between power and weakness, but according to mythic images which tempt those who have not yet taken them up, but which bring death as soon as they are assumed. Everything happens as if history were a huge galaxy of fascinating portraits reflected by mirrors.

Michel Zéraffa, *Europe*, July 1960

Illusion and reality and their conflict, and the fact that all reality is ultimately illusion, that is the basic theme of Genet's fascinating piece. It may, in some ways, be flawed as a dramatic structure, but ultimately it stands and triumphs as a great poem, an archetypal statement of man's predicament. . . . The clients of the brothel go there not just for sex. They act out their fantasies of power. . . . For, in Genet's view, ultimately sex and power are expressions of the same human drive — man's search to have an impact on his fellow human beings. . . . For these difficult and profound ideas Genet has found a magnificent theatrical sequence of images. . . . The whole play becomes an immense ritual — a sequence of stylized movements carried out as a sacred ceremonial which serves the purpose of reincarnating a metaphysical truth beyond the power of merely realistic enactment. For Genet the Mass is the most perfect form of theatre. *The Balcony* is something like a Black Mass.

Martin Esslin,
Plays and Players, Jan. 1972

What emerges most strongly from this version [Hands, 1987] is the paradoxical impulse to sacrifice individuality for the sake of some fixed and immutable role: as though life were of less value than achieving immortality as a heroic statue.

Irving Wardle, *The Times*, 16 July 1987

What is it that disturbs? Above all that which does not declare itself as disturbing. Roger Blin had clearly understood this in Genet's case: his production of *The Blacks*, playing on a sort of knowing awkwardness, escaped from the public's perpetual desire for stereotypes and kept Genet's work in that state of metaphysical disorientation which is its justification. . . . With its curtains and manageresses, Peter Brook's *Balcony* is nothing more than a play about vice as understood by right-thinking people. Genet's *Balcony* demonstrated the tragic play of essence and existence, the self and the other; it was a meditation on existential, not moral, values; its aim was to disturb the understanding of being, not good. Peter Brook's *Balcony* reduces this questioning to the petty stature of a society which is astonished to go into a brothel, to hear the mistress's worldly philosophy, to see a customer having himself whipped. All that, both remarkable and familiar, doesn't disturb any established order.

Roland Barthes, *Théâtre populaire*, April 1960

For a critic interested simply in theatrical values, Jean Genet's *The Balcony* provides a field day. For the critic interested in ideas and their place in society, it poses a problem of the first magnitude. . . . The plot is designed to convey the notion that all institutions and accepted roles of social life — politics, law, the military, government, civil authority, royalty, the church, and so on — have no more objective reality than the imaginings of perverse sexualists. . . . Thus to see the play is like being in that state when you are having a nightmare and know you are having it. I wanted to scream and wake up. But Genet claims that if you do, you wake only to more of the same nightmare. . . . The ideas of *The Balcony* are in one way reminiscent of Freud. Freud was convinced that the social forms of life are to be understood as expressions of unconscious libidinal drives. Yet ultimately Genet's view is different from Freud's because Freud regarded the social forms as 'sublimations' of the erotic forces; that is, a turning of them into socially useful and objectively desirable manifestations. In Genet's world there is no such thing as 'sublimations', since that word implies a movement from a lower to a higher plane, and thus some degree of objectivity. For Genet, there is no higher and lower, no objectivity. One mirror is as good as another, one form of illusion as useful (or useless) as another. . . . 'Why is there nothing and not something?' Watching the play after this question sprung to mind, one is filled with fear, pain, terror, and dread, and also with what I can only call an infinite metaphysical sadness. . . . The worth of *The Balcony* is that it demonstrates so triumphantly that the true nature of theatre is to reach to the level of man's ontological experience, to posit, if you will, a consistent and basic world view.

Tom F. Driver, *Christian Century*, 4 May 1960

Genet's construction is nightmarish, perverse, and chaotic as are the creations of our fantasies, but like them it has its own illuminating vividness, its lurid clarity, and a language — as intensely solid as a classic — which gives the play a substance that cuts through the darkness. . . . It retains a certain elusiveness because the emanations of the artist's unconscious project beyond the control of his will. . . . I suspect that Genet belongs to a category of artists who, while marginal to the mainstream of major work (that which possesses great duration and broad applicability), retain a certain symbolic significance for their time . . . a ferment, giving rise to what may be described as a salutary disease — through which we recognize what is happening in and troubling the epoch. . . . These artists isolate and bring into view the symptoms which threaten us. They are portents and protests.

Harold Clurman, *The Nation*, 19 March 1960

The rat-a-tat-tat of machine guns announces that religion, revolution, and the cycles of civilization have been completely redefined as purely erotic phenomena, and a rebellion is beginning outside. The Grand Balcony has become, in the short course of the evening, society, the universe, and the entire stage of history, as conceived by a cunning and diabolical mind.

Robert Brustein, *New Republic*, 28 March 1960

The whole of Genet's play, with its subtleties and crudeness, is based on the mask, the necessity of the mask — which is so universally accepted that there is no civilization which does not sanction the harsh and rather crude explosion of carnivals.

Jacques Lemarchand, *Figaro littéraire*, 21 May 1960

The playwright's genius is to have created an extremely powerful poetic language to respond to the latent and not yet articulated questioning of the meaning of individual and collective existence, since it places man's destiny no longer in the hands of the gods, but in the hands of man.

Jean Duvignaud, *Critique*, Aug.-Sept. 1957

The problem that torments the Chief of Police is indicative of one of the most important social transformations of the first half of the twentieth century: the growing prestige accorded to techniques of repression in the minds of the general public. . . . The essential subject of Genet's play is precisely that transformation: the fact that the Chief of Police will penetrate the dreams of power of those who have no power.

Lucien Goldmann, Temps modernes, June 1960

[Who exactly, then, is the hero?]

The hero of the play, if there is one, is the Chief of Police.

R.D. Laing, Self and Others (Harmondsworth: Penguin, 1971)

Roger is the real hero of *The Balcony*.

Martin Esslin, The Theatre of the Absurd
(New York: Doubleday, 1961)

For there can be no question of it: it is Irma who triumphs in this play, she alone wears the stamp of heroism.

Joseph McMahon, The Imagination of Jean Genet
(New Haven: Yale Univ. Press, 1963)

[Ambiguity of theme is perhaps best served by ambiguity of treatment on the stage.]

They [Epp, 1961] have given the play a harder edge and, to some extent, have betrayed it through adopting a crude realist, almost photographic, angle. . . . The production becomes a demonstration, whereas the play is a mad tumultuous dream, a bitter yet extravagant meditation.

Paul Morelle, Libération, 10 July 1961

Genet's theatre is a slow, dark liturgy where man pursues his own being and becomes lost, a play of reflections where the images become confused, deformed, and disappear, a threatening rite where illusion reigns. . . . Its beauty is a combination of the rigorous and the casual, a beauty forged from a detachment which requires an extremely pure mode of expression, both in its cruelty and crudity, as though everything was smooth, shiny, constant. The density has a disquieting power and gives an unforgiving hardness and sharpness to the baroque structure of the play.

Pierre Marcabru, Arts, 25 May 1960

Seldom can such a brilliant dramatic conception have been so long-windedly dissipated. . . . It's the carnival motif which gives the play its surface vitality and at the same time neutralizes its essential dramatic force: and it's as a carnival that Mr. Hands has directed it. . . . The naturalistic groundwork which is central to the play's purpose is sacrificed to an exaggerated theatricality, with the result that, for example, the Bishop's 'real life' as a gas-man loses its connection with his fantasy apotheosis. This is not, I suggest, what Genet meant at all.

Derek Mahon, *The Listener*, 9 Dec. 1971

The revolution, in the latest version presented by M. Lavaudant, loses its reality to become the supreme game offered by Mme Irma to her clients. The realistic play seen by Lucien Goldmann becomes a complete phantasmagoria where the only reality is 'The Brothel', the temple of all illusions, the theatre where, following the logic of the inversion of values, the only truth is false. . . . M. Lavaudant and M. Vergier have set themselves up as the servants of this self-enclosed religious service, this Mass without communion . . . where the audience, reduced to the role of voyeur, is present at a ritual without participating in anything.

Philippe Sénart, *Revue des deux mondes*, Jan.-March 1986

Genet's allegory is a parade of mirrors. It is a world of savage perceptions and topsy-turvy logic, graveyard humour, gutter imagery, sado-masochistic atmosphere, urchin cynicism, and, most importantly, philosophical poetry. It shocks and it dazzles, it annoys and it intrigues.

Clive Barnes, *New York Times*, 14 Dec. 1976

Genet's style does not fit into any known or recognizable style. His delirium is uncontrolled. His imagery is both weak and stunning. You are lost as he demonstrates the passage from fantasy to reality and vice versa. Scene follows scene in the greatest disorder. The characters are badly drawn. There are several possible endings. Genet is the opposite of a classic. He is a runaway horse, a torrent, a word thief who is fleeing as fast as he can, a wide-awake dreamer, a provocateur. . . . The play is a piece of baroque Pirandello or a 'Life as a Dream' without end. The sumptuousness of some costumes and props, the exaggerated make-up, the shots and explosions which wake us every now and then from this splendid nightmare, everything contrives to subject us to an exhausting vertigo. You leave the theatre groggy, unable to express what you have seen and heard. Is it a masterpiece or simply an anthology of contemporary theatre?

Guy Dumur, *Nouvel Observateur*, 27 Dec. 1985

Mr. Hands has realized that Genet communicates through images rather than ideas; and with the help of Farah's kaleidoscopic designs, he offers us a retina-ravishing spectacle. . . . The idea of the whorehouse as a symbol of the role-playing outside world has been transformed from an intellectual conceit into a moving reality.

Michael Billington, *The Guardian*, 26 Nov. 1971

This is not to say that *The Balcony* . . . is anything like a flawless masterpiece. Pirandello long ago alerted us to the fact that reality is simply another illusion. Even Genet's famous brothel setting, with its clients dressed as Bishop, Judge, and General to remind us that power and sex have the same roots, makes a fairly obvious point. . . . But what makes *The Balcony* revival is less the the quality of Genet's ideas than the theatricality of his imagination.

Michael Billington, *The Guardian*, 17 July 1987

The Balcony now has only the character of a commemorative ceremony. The anti-value of vice and disorder which used to shock (and show a profit) twenty years ago, now show themselves for what they are, the props for the stage on which we mime the last movements of the most derisory of danses macabres.

Philippe Sénart, *Revue des deux mondes*, Aug. 1975

It is somewhat sad to be disappointed. It is unpleasant to think that it is due to the evaporation of the smell of scandal which was spread by the first production. The five-star brothel and the sado-masochistic numbers are no longer strong enough to offend anyone anymore: did we admire being offended? No, rather it is because the fantasies of the middle-class customers . . . ridiculed values that were still respected. Genet was attacking still-living myths then. What is he attacking today? Nothing other than myths that have already been rejected.

Raymonde Temkine, *Europe*, March 1986

Genet never falters while he is creating his horrifying world of fantasy, built up by savage rituals which have a perverse fascination and beauty of their own. But when he comes to the more mundane matter of practical government he fails. His power is the power of the poet to evoke an imaginary world: faced by reality he lacks the cold logical mind to offer us enlightenment. Having disturbed us by the force of his imagination, he is unable to resolve the questions he has raised in our minds.

Frank Granville Barker, *Plays and Players*, June 1957

[Disturbing for the audience, the play is equally difficult for the actors.]

Actor Robert Bernal [The Archbishop] . . . was so worried about the script that he asked a priest whether he should appear. He was told there was no religious objection.

Edward Goring, *Daily Mail*, 8 April 1957

The constant breaking of rhythm and style is very difficult for an actor who is tempted to give himself up to the classical spirit. *The Balcony* is exactly that. A classical actor is lost. But a cinema actor or a good light comedy actor, for opposite reasons, is equally lost. When I was looking for actors to play *The Balcony,* it happened that, for the first time in my life, I had to deal with excellent actors who refused good parts. For the first time as well I heard and saw shocked actors telling me: 'No. I can't act in this play.'

Peter Brook, *L'Express*, 19 May 1960

[Directors have had the additional difficulty of dealing with the author who, for example, tried to halt the 1957 production by occupying the stage until an injunction prevented him from entering the theatre.]

The violence of castration, rebellion, flagellation on the stage; the violence of the collision between author and director, between author and management; the violence of popular revulsion, of the sensation surrounding the opening night — all were subordinate to the violent clash, in real life, between fantasy and reality, both in the author's mind and, during every performance, in the minds of the audience. . . . Genet, whose main preoccupation is with the ambiguous boundary between fantasy and reality, had been disillusioned when he realized the distance separating his vision of the play from its realization. . . . Genet's great importance in the theatre is his theatricality. He does not 'use' the theatre to imitate the externals of our world; he shows us that our world is as false as grease-paint itself, and that therefore the theatre can be the perfect mirror held up to the *danse macabre* which is life as Genet sees it. In other words, Genet's theatre at its best, abstract, stylized, deliberately stagey, comes closer to penetrating reality than the illusionist theatre ever did. In *The Balcony* and, to a lesser extent, in *The Maids*, Genet gives back to the theatre a vital quality which it has not had since the religious drama of the Middle Ages. He gives back the quality of ritual, of ceremony. He does not do this externally as some twentieth-century verse drama has attempted to do, but by putting on stage the very ceremonies, be they sexual or religious, that he sees being performed in real life. I have been asked on several occasions what *The Balcony* says. It is not a play that *says*; it is a play that *sees*.

Peter Zadek, *New Statesman*, 4 May 1957

When I had *The Balcony* in my hands, I discovered a poet who, as Cocteau would say, wrote 'poetry of the stage', a poet who, starting from a sense of rigour and a rejection of naturalism, strove to discover forms to express what he experienced and what he thought. With Genet, we arrive at a purely traditional and deeply classical form of theatre, but one which is conceived with a totally new passion and violence.

Peter Brook, *L'Express*, 19 May 1960

Rather I would see it as a great allegory on the history of the inter-war years which the play tries to surpass by asking existential questions and in which Being and Seeming, Death and Reflection, dig enormous metaphysical and meta-historical holes.

Georgio Strehler, *Il Corriere della Sera*, 20 May 1976

[Genet has been particularly acerbic about productions of this play.]

Mr. Zadek is an imbecile. He has introduced a sensational element into the play. There is no nobility about Mr. Zadek's brothel. It is vulgar, cheap. The splendour is missing.

Genet, to Robert Muller, *Picture Post*, 11 May 1957

The true theme of the play is illusion. Everything is false: the General, the Archbishop, the Chief of Police, and everything should be treated with the utmost delicacy. Now, instead of making the play noble, it was vulgarized. The characters became disgusting and grotesque puppets that I didn't even recognize. . . . I wanted characters who were larger than life. They have made them into Helzapoppin-like caricatures. If *The Maids* and *Deathwatch* are now performed badly, it is not important, for I know these plays have been performed well and what their potential is, but *The Balcony* was being put on for the first time and I was beside myself with anger for having been the father of this monster.

Genet, *L'Express*, 26 April 1957

Unlike what happened in Paris, the Three Figures (Bishop, Judge, General) will be dressed in uniforms or clothes that are current in the country where the play is being performed. In France, it was essential to have a judge who looked like a judge from our court of assizes, not a bewigged judge; the General needed to have a kepi with stars or oak leaves round it, not the headgear of a Lord Admiral. The costumes should be exaggerated, but not unrecognizable. . . .

One more thing: do not perform this play as if it were a satire on this or that. It is — and therefore is to be played as — the glorification of The Image and its Reflection. Its meaning — be it satirical or not — will only become clear if this is the case.

Genet, 'Comment jouer *Le Balcon*',
in *Le Balcon* (Décines: L'Arbalète, 1962)

The Blacks (Les Nègres)

Written: began 1955, renamed *Football* in 1956; Blin started work with Les Griots in Feb. 1958.

First production: Théâtre de Lutèce, Paris, 28 Oct. 1959 (dir. Roger Blin).

First American production: St. Mark's Playhouse, New York, 4 May 1961 (dir. Gene Frankel).

First British production: Royal Court Theatre, 30 May 1961 (dir. Roger Blin).

Major revivals: Oxford Playhouse, Oxford, 20 Jan. 1970 (dir. Minos Volanakis); Iva Aldridge Theater, Washington, D.C., April, 1971 (dir. Vera J. Katz); Eisenhower Theater, Washington, D.C., 26 May 1973 (dir. Robert Hooks); Schaubuhne, Berlin, 24 June 1983 (dir. Peter Stein); Théâtre du Port de la Lune, Bordeaux, 1988 (dir. Jean-Louis Thamin).

First published: Décines: L'Arbalète, 1958; a second edition appeared in 1960 with 33 photos of the production and Genet's note 'Pour jouer Les Nègres'.

Translation: as *The Blacks: a Clown Show,* translated by Bernard Frechtman, with some textual variants, New York: Grove; London: Faber, 1960. A new English version commissioned by the Royal Shakespeare Company from Wole Soyinka in 1987 is unpublished.

Before a court of white-masked blacks, a troupe of fellow blacks act out the story of Village's murder of a white female victim, now lying in a catafalque centre-stage. Archibald, the leader of the troupe, struggles to keep the ceremony moving forward. The account of the murder is clouded and diverted by interjections from the court, eruptions of jealousy between Virtue and Snow, professions of love from Village and Virtue, and highly mannered verbal battles between the White Queen and Mrs. Felicity. The shaky progress of the ceremony is further disturbed by messages brought by Newport News from off-stage where another trial is reportedly being conducted. The catafalque on stage is revealed to be no more than two missing chairs, whereas the reports from off-stage describe the conviction of a black traitor and the emergence of a new leader. However, the curtain falls on the troupe reassembling around another catafalque at the back of the stage, suggesting the start of another ceremony. The play between the reality and appearance of the on-stage and off-stage action finds its reflection in the situation in the theatre: blacks performing a ceremony for an audience of false whites on-stage, but the whole troupe performing a clown show for an audience of real whites in the auditorium. This intricate and seamless dramatic fabric is coloured by recurrent thematic strands: a parody of colonial power, the relationship between black and white in a post-colonial period, the clash of black and white cultures, the relationship between political liberation and freedom, and the nature of blackness itself.

[The critics assumed their customary opposing positions; the more conservative reacted vituperatively to the perceived attack on their values; the more liberal saluted a major theatrical achievement.]

It cannot be denied that this spell-binding but prolix spectacle succeeds on a physical level and that it wins the wager of being sincere while betraying the consummate artificiality of its means of expression.

Georges Lerminier, *Parisien libéré*, 7 Nov. 1959

Everything is clarified, raised, sublimated by an unreproachable magical style, by such a tonal quality, by such a dramatic intensity that even the most obviously crude utterances, suffused with a poetic glow, seem necessary.

Paul Morelle, *Libération*, 4 Nov. 1959

It is impossible to describe what happens in this play, firstly because of the improbable, but certainly deliberate, confusion in which what we can hardly call the action unfolds. . . . Don't let us think that it is the true, deepest Africa which is revealed to us by a white writer whom everyone knows to be corrupt to the core. That would be a bad joke. What is expressed in Genet's work is a totally rootless underworld whose origin is to be found in the nightclubs of Montmartre or Pigalle. Genet doesn't just utter, he spits out, he vomits out the denial of all that is honorable and worthy in the Christian west, and he replaces it with a deliberately maintained confusion between what is irreproachably good in the civilizing process and the abuses and excesses which nobody would deny nor excuse.

Gabriel Marcel, *Nouvelles littéraires*, 17 Dec. 1959

We are invited to a festival of poetry, but we end up at a flower-arranging competition. Because of his volubility, his ridiculous stridency, Jean Genet hardly rises above the workaday writers who strive to reinvent a style which already sounded false at the time of the troubadours. . . . His pleading curses, his insults, are not the products of an inspired mind or a high-minded rebel but rather the outpourings from a mean and petty revolt or a truly puerile annoyance.

Georges Portal, *Ecrits de Paris*, Sept. 1960

It lacks the authentic voice with which Africa stirs hope and faith. The blacks provide the accessories to the savage carnival. Any philosophic ideas are due to M. Jean-Paul Sartre; the rest are the commonplaces of the most conformist non-conformity, with all the necessary 'antis': anti-colonialism, anti-clericalism, anti-militarism. . . . It's a *pièce à thèse*, an Aunt Sally where the player is sure to win every time.

Henri Gouhier, *La Table ronde*, Feb. 1960

After the impenetrable thickets of Mr. Genet's verbiage, you'll lust for the elegant ease of Ionesco, the chummy accessibility of Beckett, the crystal clarity of Pinter.

Robert Muller, *Daily Mail*, 31 May 1961

The Blacks is one of those plays that circles round, living off its own tail; Ionesco (shall we say?) but weighed down all too explicitly with heavy ideas about ritual and the unconscious, cheapened by crude satire and lacking his art. . . . Genet is dabbling cleverly in the genuine raw material of the African imagination. The trouble is that, in the manner of the Boulevard Saint Germain, he is taking things from his imagination, formalizing them, and re-issuing them as ideas: not hating, but Hatred; not killing, but Murder as purgation, as necessary self-fulfilment, or as political principle.

V. S. Pritchett, *New Statesman*, 9 June 1961

His theatre . . . like his philosophy, seems to me so negative as to get us nowhere. . . . If Genet's purpose is to make us rethink from the very beginning every conception that we hold concerning ourselves and the world about us, then it has validity. But if he cannot let fall one crumb of positive thought, is not one play enough? Or are we expected to go on admiring the undeniable skill with which he presents his problems in theatrical algebra knowing all the time their author will never hint at the shadow of a solution?

Frank Granville Barker, *Plays and Players*, July 1961

[The appropriateness of Genet's nihilism and theatrical ingenuity in the context of a play dealing with race is a recurring theme of critical comment.]

Les Nègres is a kind of Black Mass in which all values are parodied and turned, rigorously although not systematically, inside out. The action is bewildering but typical of all Genet's plays. They are always done with mirrors. He has one theme only: the impossibility of ever separating appearance from reality. With this excuse he has managed to dramatize all his personal tics and preoccupations. In *The Maids* it was a preoccupation with class: who is the servant? In *The Balcony* it was fame, prestige, influence. . . . In *The Blacks* it is the antipathy and eternal misunderstandings of black and white. So superficially it might seem that Genet is climbing out of his narrow world into the grander, wider skies of contemporary problems. But not at all. When he calls the piece a 'clownerie', he knows what he is about. The obscenity and Groucho Marxism that rage throughout are no measured, Sartrean statement about the colour problem. On the contrary, the play seems written out of anger and a sense of absurdity. . . . He piles on blasphemy on blasphemy, contradiction on contradiction, in the hope of reducing the whole infuriating order of things to rubble. It is the theatre of nihilism, which relies for its effect not on any depth of implication but on some stylish clowning at the very edge of sense, on the author's occasionally magnificent gift of the gab and odd moments of surprisingly mannered wit.

A. Alvarez, *New Statesman*, 21 Nov. 1959

So far from being 'written out of anger and a sense of absurdity' the play seems to me . . . to address itself to the errors and aspirations of both sides in Africa with a compassionate understanding which restores to the theatre something of its ancient stature as the interpreter of human destiny. So far from being 'the theatre of nihilism' it has much which is wise and constructive to say about the problem which will arise as one domination gives place to another. . . . The lesson of the play, as of what is happening now in Africa, is that the old order of things will be reduced to rubble, whether we like it or not; and that what matters is that the new order should offer fewer affronts to human dignity.

Vera Lindsay, *New Statesman*, 28 Nov. 1959

[There is no unanimity over the effect, or indeed the breadth, of Genet's social criticism.]

M. Jean Genet has used all his poetic power, which is great, to put colonialism on trial. . . . Beyond the monotonous passages, the numerous redundancies in the dialogue, we are presented with a real miracle which took our breath away, which alternately threw us into pits of despair and raised us to the heights of joy.

Pierre Berger, *Paris Jours*, 4 Nov. 1959

A 'clown show' which takes your breath away for two hours (without an interval), which for eight days makes you think sanely about the evil, the successor to slavery, that is racism. This play, which remains rooted in your mind, even if it is embellished with puns, outrageous yet deliberate statements, is great theatre. . . . Jean Genet has achieved a *tour de force* in writing this play that real blacks have made their own and which they brandish like the flag of their reconquered dignity.

Anonymous, *Droit et liberté*, Nov. 1959

Genet probes into the minds of both blacks and whites, the oppressed and the oppressors, revealing the latent resentment of the former and the latter's defensive platitudes. He is on the side of the blacks, articulating their mutinous feelings that have not yet reached the level of conscious protest. An objective observer might say that Genet makes a case loaded in favour of the blacks. It is difficult, however, to hold on to one's calmness and objectivity at a performance. . . . Adequate appreciation of *The Blacks*, if it is possible, requires some knowledge of the history of colonialism, its benevolence and atrocities, guided by an alert intelligence. Otherwise the gallimaufry of indecencies, mockery of religious values, anti-colonialist propaganda, and interracial idealism doesn't make sense. As performed at St. Marks, it doesn't have to make sense. It simply stuns the audience with its emotional impact.

Theophilus Lewis, *America*, 25 Aug. 1961

Jean Genet subtitled his play, depicting the revolution of the blacks against white civilization, 'a clown show'. . . . He advances on racism from many fronts: linguistic, conceptual, histrionic, mythic. The drama is a parody of a ritual, in which clowning and derision demonstrate the bitterness and sarcasm of the play.

Doug Arthur, *Educational Theatre Journal*, Oct. 1972

The asocial outcast, Jean Genet, hits us in the face with wads of bitter images which range from clowning to pleadings, from blasphemy to pure poetry, but which together through parody put western civilization on trial. . . . Caught in the swell of language, we are really witnessing ourselves on trial, our beliefs, our cultures and that which we hold most dear.

Robert Abirached, *Etudes*, Jan. 1960

The Blacks accommodates a powerful satire on white supremacy, imperialist attitudes, and cultural pretensions, showing the ruling class blending fatuity with authority and hypocritical benevolence with condescending superiority. . . . I do not know of a more devastating play (its satirical animosity is blistering) in the recent repertoire of the avant-garde. . . . It creates a state of anarchy that challenges all values, disturbs all peace of mind, and upbraids all encrustations of socially acceptable sentiment. . . . It is not a play that achieves penetration and illumination as its final result, for the mind stops understanding the work under mesmerization even when it is not distracted by confusion or irritation. And the same thing can be said about the emotional end result: . . . the work is so drastically cathartic that it is not actually purging, for it produces new tensions and leaves one groggy from the assault on the nervous system. The result may well be that a work of tremendous honesty of emotion that makes short shrift of traffic with social bromides becomes in effect sensational and self-defeating.

John Gassner, *Educational Theatre Journal*, Oct. 1961

For two and a half hours we hear a provocative, terrible frenzy of spell-binding, poetic words which abruptly changes rhythm, with extra-ordinary moments and some monotonous passages which abuse and stifle the audience. . . . I don't believe that this play can be of any assistance to Africans in their long and continuing struggle to have those who don't want to, recognize their claim to human and social dignity.

Andrée Clair, *Présence africaine*, Feb.-Mar. 1960

The play certainly has validity in its purgation of the whites (in the audience) but what I found to be its spectacular quality of detachment for the blacks (in the audience) must surely be a limitation which derives from the fact that, for all of its sophistication, it is itself an expression of some of the more quaint notions of white men.

Lorraine Hansberry, *Village Voice*, 1 June 1961

To appreciate fully the play's quality one would have to be taking part in it, caught up oneself in the conflicting moods of the ritual. Genet wants the white audience to become involved in the ritual through being deeply affronted . . . but this is extremely unlikely to happen in any sophisticated and liberal city. For the audience to fill their proper role in *The Blacks*, the play would have to be performed in Nairobi and, indeed, to have been written by Kenyatta.

Bamber Gascoigne, *The Spectator*, 9 June 1961

The Blacks is in no way a sepia-tinted picture intended to illustrate the colonial record. Rather, the play brings out the fundamental mis-understandings which, above and beyond the obvious abuses and most glaring mutual wrongs, seem to preclude the coming together of races. However, does Genet not mix things up? Many have commented on the Pirandellism of his technique, indeed on the double meaning of his lyricism. All this will never have the harrowing force of the most spontaneous negro spiritual. This poetic game-playing is still in the 'white' manner, the sophisticated 'white' manner.

Georges Lerminier, *Pensée française*, April 1960

So with the action. One has a group of negroes who are revolutionaries. They commit a ritual murder each night. But they are also players who entertain a world of White leaders, mounted literally above them on the stage. They are in subservience to them, yet they are not. For the audience never can quite forget that the Whites are really Blacks-in-White-masks. One is asked to consider a theme which may be the central moment of the twentieth century: the passage of power from the White to those he oppressed. But this theme is presented in such a web of formal contradictions and formal turns sufficiently complex to be a play in itself.

Pirandello never made this mistake. His dance of mirrors was always built on pretexts which were flimsy. If one's obsession is with the contradictory nature of reality, the audience must be allowed to dispense with the superficial reality in order to explore its depths. The foreground of *The Blacks* is too oppressive. One cannot ignore it. White and Black in mortal confrontation are far more interesting than the play of shadows that Genet brings to it.

Norman Mailer, *Village Voice*, 18 May 1961

[For several critics a strictly anti-colonialist/black-versus-white interpretation is too narrow.]

There are those who would interpret *The Blacks* as simply a burning
indictment of white society and white inhumanity. But isn't the virtue of
this play the fact that it is unrelated to political or social policy. . . . If
Mr. Genet is plumping for anything in this play, it is perhaps for a
destruction of a sentimental and hypocritical society that happens to be
white, in favour of a more cruel and realistic society that happens to be
black. He also indicates, however, that such a shift in power is more
likely to come about from white exhaustion than black militancy and
that it might result in a society just as squeamish and ignoble as he feels
the present one to be. Thus *The Blacks* is a porcupine with quills of
sharp paradox aimed at anyone who would embrace it.

Henry Hewes, *Saturday Review*, 3 June 1961

I don't think that one now would be as likely to interpret the play's
theme as one stating that blacks are superior to whites; one now tunes
into the much more universal one — that Genet was hitting at all forms
of hypocrisy. It merely happens that these are blacks, Africans, pitted
against European whites. . . . It is not so much the black-white conflict
which arrests our attention as the injustice of misused power.

Richard L. Coe, *Washington Post*, 28 May 1973

The trouble is, of course, that Genet did not really write a play about
racial discrimination and its effects on its victims. *The Blacks* is another
expression of Genet's anarchist love of mayhem, and it needs a highly
informative programme note about present-day conditions in Africa for
us to accept that the celebration of underdog violence should be considered for a political demonstration.

Michael Stone, *The Guardian*, 24 June 1983

It is clear in the development of the ambivalent relation between blacks
and whites that the 'race problem' is only one of a complex of
dialectical pairs in which black serves as a symbol for the sacrality of
the Negative. The drama of *The Blacks* is thus the drama of the 'rejected
zone' whether of the psyche, or of society, or of the dominant
civilization: it is the zone of the 'totally other', of the repressed.

Susan Taubes, *Tulane Drama Review*, Spring 1963

It is based . . . on the recurrent Genetic idea that all human relationships
are power relationships. There are those who dominate and those who

are dominated; and the process whereby the two factions exchange roles corresponds to the systole and diastole of history. . . . His theme in *The Blacks* is the hatred of the Negro for the ruling Caucasian, which we may take to symbolize the hatred of all despised outsiders for the society that spurns them. . . . The subject cries out for the dry passion of a satirist, a Swift of the theatre, a theatrical vivisectionist; instead, it drowns in a flood of prose poetry. Genet's mind moves from image to image, never from idea to idea. . . . The images pile up, some of them memorable, others merely capricious; meanwhile, the argument stands still.

Kenneth Tynan, *The Observer*, 1 June 1961

The Blacks is a depth charge of evil which sinks the spectator well below the placid surface of social benevolence to the dark sea floor of the unconscious, leaving him totally submerged beneath a torrent of primitive impulses, sado-masochistic hallucinations, and myths of danger. . . . Genet has a Pirandellian obsession with the idea that human identity is defined by play-acting; and *The Blacks* . . . examines the artificiality of human behaviour in a world of rigid definitions. But whereas this philosophical probing enriched the vision of sham in *The Balcony*, it merely muddies the ritualistic line of *The Blacks*. . . . Because of Genet's failure to integrate his conscious preoccupations with his unconscious fantasies, *The Blacks* remains an elusive enigma. But while it fails as a philosophical drama, it stands triumphant as a cruel purgative myth, enlivened by a fierce imagination, a rich theatrical sense, and some of the most superb imagery in all modern drama.

Robert Brustein, *New Republic*, 29 May 1961

[Neither has the play's structure satisfied all who have seen it, though in France some critics have been more tolerant towards the non-linear complexities of its conception.]

But as the evening takes one more step, in its second act, it does not mean to take the step that ancient man and the ancient theatre actually took — the step into defined meaning, into controlled illumination. It simply slips back, slavering rather, breathing hard and refusing the effort at conscious shaping, the struggle towards intelligibility. In the circumstances, and in spite of all there is to be grateful for, we find ourselves dissatisfied.

Walter Kerr, *New York Herald Tribune*, 14 May 1961

By having a play performed by some of the actors in front of the others dressed as whites within the play itself, by multiplying the dramatic illusion by distancing the audience from what is happening on stage, Genet has created a form of poetic theatre, a closed space, an absolute, in which an occult ceremony unfolds, hidden from the eyes of the world and dedicated to the glory of a secret language. . . . The mixture in *The Blacks* of comedy and tragedy, religious rite and play, farce and lyricism, grace and obscenity recalls the best plays of Lorca. It's magic theatre whose fragrance must be allowed to impregnate you slowly.

Dominique Fernandez, *Nouvelle Revue française*, 1 Jan. 1960

It is impossible to swallow it like a predigested product of western humanism or like an inoffensive pill. This is a form of theatre which makes you scream, which summons up demons. For the first time, it shows the possibility of the famous theatre of cruelty which still haunts us in spite of Brecht's pronouncements. In short, a theatre that should not leave you untouched. . . . Theatre, mysticism, and prohibited sexuality, such is the trilogy which marks with an exquisite smell of decay this work of quirky reflections and noxious scents, this theatre in which an indissoluble union of baroque affectation and filth guarantees a paradoxical victory for poetry. . . . The leader of the troupe harangues the audience in the theatre not to include it in the action, but to exclude it so that it is conscious of being a disapproving spectator. . . . The black is acting with his own inner, malefic self, not with an invented character which would seek to be taken as reality. . . . It is this determination not to deceive on the level of *re-presentation* which creates before our eyes the theatre and its double, because everything is clearly marked with immediacy. . . . It has to be said that it is hardly bearable. Only poetry can save such a theatre from its own traps, and that's what happens with this play.

Alfred Simon, *Esprit*, Jan. 1960

At the end of the play, what is left for the white reader or member of the audience? The infinitely proud, but also infinitely miserable feeling of being apart, and excluded from the ceremony which has just taken place: the overwhelming recognition of the white's loneliness and banishment from the colour black.

Jean Cau, *L'Express*, 20 Feb. 1958

There is no sense of representation on the stage . . . as we watch the play, watch the identities and roles slide from player to player . . . we finally get a sense that the players are particular people who have chosen to speak to us this evening and that they are different from us . . . as we sit there we are assaulted by the players. . . . And so the performance ends; the contest which is not a contest between black and white ends. There has been no communication, nothing transmitted, no new message, nothing but an evening of emptiness and solitude after which we walked slowly back to the subway, looking suspiciously at everyone who looked at us.

Thomas Taylor, *Players Magazine*, Oct. 1964

[On the other side of the footlights the play has proved to be equally challenging.]

Yes, it's something like that for us. A great release. To think of being able to act out to the hilt, on a stage, in front of everybody, all that has gone to give us our prejudices. . . . It's an undreamed of opportunity.

Robert Liensol (Ville de Saint-Nazaire), to Maria Craipeau, *France Observateur*, 22 Oct. 1959

Genet, the black white, feels he is more intelligent than those who punish him or could punish him, and he is refined enough to take his revenge through refinement. The actors realized this: they understood that he was a black white and they experienced the jubilation that I felt myself and want to pass on to the public. . . . This insolent rejoicing shocked certain actors, for example the actress who left the company rather than say 'my mother shat me out standing up'.

Roger Blin, to Jean Duvignaud, *Lettres nouvelles*, 28 Oct. 1959

[The dramatic effect of the play is intimately linked to the presence of blacks on the stage and whites in the auditorium.]

The play is a politicized Black Mass: a statement both of Negro hatred and an oppressed people's ironic readiness to conform to the white man's stereotyped image. And Stein's production brings out, better than anything since Victor Garcia's *The Maids*, Genet's delight in ritual. . . . [Yet] there is something faintly disquieting about seeing white actors paying vicarious homage to black power, even something politically simplistic since the production takes no account of Africa's post-colonial history. Deep down, I think *The Blacks* needs to be played by blacks. How else do you get the rich irony of actors mimicking negroes as imagined by whites? How else do you get the faint thrill of apprehension when a white spectator is enticed on stage to become part of the ritual?

Michael Billington, *The Guardian*, 19 Oct. 1984

[Genet has expressed his own views on casting and the conditions of performance. Only latterly did he allow productions that did not comply with these views.]

You can well understand that if, a few days before their execution, men under sentence of death — real ones — could, in the presence of their judges and executioners, perform, in the prison yard, a play dealing with the perfidious relations between themselves and their judges and executioners, the dramatic emotion arising out of such a performance would have nothing in common with what usually happens in the theatre. Now it happens that the Blacks — the real ones — are under a weighty sentence delivered by a weighty tribunal, Whites — also real ones. These Blacks are thus in the situation indicated in the image I used above: real condemned men in the presence of judges and executioners. . . . Any Negro performer can act in my play, anywhere, without my permission: to that extent, it no longer belongs to me. But you must certainly realize that the drama would cease to exist in the hall if white actors, made up as blacks, appeared on stage instead of real blacks speaking out their real miseries.

> Jean Genet, 'To a Would-Be Producer',
> *Tulane Drama Review*, Spring 1963

The play, written, I repeat, by a white man, is intended for a white audience, but if — which is unlikely — it is ever performed before a black audience, then a white person, male or female, should be invited every evening. The organizer of the show should welcome him formally, dress him in ceremonial costume and lead him to his seat, preferably in the front row of the stalls. The actors will play for him. A spotlight should be focused upon this symbolic white throughout the performance.

> Jean Genet, Foreword to *The Blacks* (London: Faber, 1967)

[Genet remains guarded over his understanding of the play.]

I write plays in order to crystallize a dramatic, theatrical emotion. I am not worried if, for example, *The Blacks* may be useful to the blacks. I don't think that it is.

> Genet, to Pierre Déméron, *Candide*, 25 April 1966

One evening an actor asked me to write a play for an all-black cast. But what exactly is a black? First of all, what's his colour?

> Genet, Note to *The Blacks* (London: Faber, 1967)

The Screens (Les Paravents)

Written: 1955-56; first referred to as *La pièce sur l'Arabe*, then as *La Mère*, and also *Ça bouge encore*.

First production: Schlosspark Theater, Berlin-Stelglitz, 19 May 1961 (dir. Hans Lietzau, using about two-thirds of printed text).

First British production: Donmar Rehearsal Rooms, London, 4 May 1964 (dir. Peter Brook and Charles Marowitz, using first 12 scenes, in front of an invited audience).

First full production: Alleteatern, Stockholm, Summer 1964 (dir. Per Carlssen).

First French production: Odéon-Théâtre de France, Paris, 16 April 1966 (dir. Roger Blin).

First American production: Chelsea Theatre Center, New York, 30 Nov. 1971 (dir. Minos Volanakis).

Major revivals: Bristol Old Vic, Bristol, 20 March 1973 (dir. Walter Donohue, a pared-down version using nine actors, adapted by Howard Brenton); Théâtre des Amandiers, Nanterre, 20 Sept. 1983 (dir. Patrice Chéreau).

Publication: Décines: L'Arbalète, 1961; a second edition with variants, Décines: L'Arbalète, 1976; reprinted, with commentaries on each scene and performance instructions, in *Oeuvres complètes*, Vol. V (Paris: Gallimard, 1979).

Translation: by Bernard Frechtman, New York: Grove, 1962; London: Faber, 1963.

This is in all respects a complex work. Its 17 scenes call for 98 characters and require four levels of performance on which a host of movable screens are used to define a multitude of settings. There are three main narrative threads: the epic of the Algerian war, Saïd's journey to oblivion, and the fate of Warda the brothel-keeper. The story of the Algerian war begins with scenes depicting the social life of a village in which Genet bitterly satirizes colonialist and militarist attitudes as well as the exploitation of the indigenous people. There are signs throughout that simmering unrest is becoming more open: the labourers burn Sir Harold's orange grove; his pig-skin glove is losing its power to control his workforce. Open conflict finally breaks out: the colonial way of life is challenged by the anarchic hatred of the people, as voiced by Kadidja. In the final scenes, there emerges an armed Algerian army. It represents the new order

*against which Ommu, as Kadidja's successor, Saïd, and Warda
carry on their individual rebellions.*

*Saïd's story, which figures strongly at the beginning and at
the end of the play, could be considered the backbone of the plot.
Apolitical and destitute, Saïd and his mother are the poorest
Arabs in the village. As a result, Saïd seeks out the ugliest
woman, the hooded Leila, for his wife. Economically and socially
marginalized, this family resort to petty crime. Unable to escape
humiliation and rejection at the hands of the muslim community,
they decide to stimulate it by striking out on a path of hatred,
evil, and isolation — a path which leads Saïd to an act of treason
against his community, and the Mother to the murder of a French
soldier. In the realm of the Dead this act brings her recognition,
but she is dismayed to learn that the living wish to honour her for
her patriotism. For his part, Saïd returns to the village where
Ommu wishes to turn him into an emblem of struggle; the new
Algerian fighters are even willing to forgive him his act of
treason if he changes his pursuit of a subversive isolation. Saïd is
shot escaping from these demands. However, like Leila, he does
not reappear in the realm of the Dead. It is suggested that he
lives on as a song — the play itself?*

*Warda's fate in some respects shadows Saïd's. At the outset,
her brothel is a place of evil and escape from reality for her
clients. Warda herself has striven to become a symbol, a deified
sexual object devoid of content, at whose skirt hems men wor-
ship. With the progress of the rebellion, the brothel becomes
utilitarian, a centre for the relief of the sexual urges of battle-
weary fighters. Warda sees her glamour and mystery being
dissipated. Rather than connive with this process, she rips her
clothes and antagonizes the women of the village. She is, in turn,
killed by their knitting needles. Thus, she retains her authenticity,
while, with order restored, her brothel assumes once more its
original function under the direction of her former assistant,
Malika.*

[The violence that surrounded the 1957 production of *The Balcony* was
as nothing compared to the demonstrations that greeted the Paris
premiere of *Les Paravents*. Both in and around the theatre, seats, smoke
bombs, and bottles were hurled in protest. The words of even the most
hostile critics are mild by comparison.]

It is possible that Jean Genet wished in *The Screens* to paint a fresco of the Algerian war. For, contrary to what has been claimed, it is not about some vague battle here or there, but clearly about a precise, localized drama; a thousand and one details in the show would have to have been forgotten in order to maintain the opposite.

It is possible that Genet intended to show the absurdities of such struggles and how hatred is born, and the wrongs of colonialism, the grave errors of our representatives, the Arab mentality, the folly of each and finally the misery of all, this misery which will continue and which is, after all, the lot of the human condition.

It's possible.

I could not argue with it.

The author's mode of expression makes me totally impervious to his intentions.

Everything in me revolts, rebels. His thoughts, what he thinks of, the instincts which motivate him, the choice of images, his patent predilection for all that is most ugly, dirty, vulgar, the cartload of waste which he delights in tipping over us, the self-satisfaction he takes in multiplying the offensive, unseemly actions, the happiness he feels in stirring up indecency, in wallowing in blasphemy, in embracing obscenity and in spitting in the face of the public only to see it swoon in adoration, all of this has an awful stench and reflects the desire, the will, the ambition, the resolution to besmirch, debase, and degrade everything.

Jean-Jacques Gautier, *Figaro*, 23 April 1966

What is not acceptable is that the French army be presented as a rabble of stupid animals, of sadists, of torturers. . . . There's worse still: the incitement not only to murder but to commit the most execrable infamies, all manner of mutilations, reverberates here as a vengeful exhortation. . . . Unfortunately there is not just the spectacle, there is the language, which is quite the most vulgar, the most systematically excremental that has ever been heard on a French stage. . . . There is also the most extreme and insulting nihilism that has ever found form in a literary work.

Gabriel Marcel, *Nouvelles littéraires*, 21 April 1966

[Away from the storm, others express dissatisfaction.]

These preliminary glimpses smacked of the most grandiose infantility. . . . It's an endless bundle of fun, except that the poetry is laid on with a dirty great trowel, and the dramatic value is nil. Only the boredom amounts to cruelty.

Roger Gellert, *New Statesman*, 31 Jan. 1964

When a writer is at a loss for anything fresh to say, he sometimes cannibalizes successful works of his own or cribs outright from someone else. In *The Screens*, Jean Genet does both. Thinly disguised furnishings of *The Balcony*, with its bordello fantasies, and *The Blacks*, with its racial voodoo masks, go floating past in this five-hour play that most nearly resembles a broiling, debris-cluttered river in flood. *The Screens*, however, lacks the cast *versus* outcast tensions of *The Blacks* and the musky eroticism of *The Balcony*. In a Genetic mutation of Bertolt Brecht, the playwright doubly fails. He tries to apply the epical veneer of *The Caucasian Chalk Circle* to the theme of the little people whipped about in a historical convulsion, in this case France's punitive struggle with Algeria. Brecht succeeded because he had a certain sympathy for the last-ditch valor of his little people even when he portrayed them as cagey sneaks. Genet fails because he regards all people as maggots.

What is original in the play — its scrambled, meandering documentary account of the Algerian war — is almost worse than what is borrowed. . . . The flaw is in the script's grandiose pretensions, which dwarf interest in any individual. . . . The language of the play is unrelentingly anal. As no great surprise, Genet finally advocates acts of evil as the only liberating force either against the old order or the new.

T. E. Kalem, *Time*, 17 Dec. 1971

[Back in France the debate is whether the play is simply an attack on the French in Algeria, or whether the situation is being used for other ends.]

This time Genet has had to deploy the tricks of an often abstruse language by using an incantatory style, a ritual inspired by Greek theatre in order to put across without violent protests, this outrage against the French in Algeria. Under the pretext of combating hypocrisy he wallows in filth. . . . There are too many wounds still bleeding for this picture of a decaying France and Algeria to be passively accepted.

André Rivollet, *Juvénal*, 22 April 1966

It is evident that the play puts colonialism on trial, but as the work of a poet, the argument has a metaphysical dimension: the enemies before us are two versions of the same human nature, distressed, separated, and torn asunder by the play of appearances.

Pierre Kyria, *Combat*, 12 April 1966

An Algerian could have seen in it the negation of several years of effort, of bloody struggle and could have been angered at the sight of a revolution being reduced to a pantomine. Neither the text nor the play show any trace of this. The play is beautiful. It hits out, it shocks, it disturbs as any literary work should do. . . . The author espouses, without reservation, the cause of independence against colonialism. Clearly it is a lesser evil since it is better than bourgeois acceptance. There doesn't seem to be a good cause. In a word, Genet's play is neither a piece of Brecht nor of Kateb Yacine. . . . The play is a sort of hymn to evil, totally without any humanism. The Algerian conflict is just an opportunity, a pretext. Moreover there is no evidence anywhere of a stand or a commitment concerning the conflict.

Lamine, *Algérien en Europe*, 1 May 1966

[The centrality of a political theme, or at least its clarity, were questioned after the Berlin production.]

To reduce the work to the level of an attack on colonialism would be to betray its possible meaning. . . . The co-existence after death of old enemies in a limbo-like state is undoubtedly Genet's deepest message. May it not be long before Paris offers us a work which will disorientate equally as much M. de Sévigny and M. Benbella — unless it should convert them both to a fascinated contemplation of an eternal elsewhere.

A. C., *Le Monde*, 18-19 June 1961

But if he seems to have written the political play that some of his critics have demanded of him, he has done it in his own peculiar, uncompromising manner. He has compounded once more his typical blending of violence and lyricism, but he has totally rejected — or, rather, defied — the idea of a crystal-clear political play that spells out every idea and makes every thought intelligible to the slowest member of the audience. As usual, M. Genet has gone his own way. *Les Paravents* is frequently brilliant in its fashion, but it is more diffuse and more difficult than any of its predecessors.

'Berlin Introduces Genet's Play about Algeria',
The Times, 26 June 1961

[There are those who believe that any political interpretations cloud the true experience of the play, others that as a political play it is unsuccessful, or that for revolution it may be better to read revolt.]

When it was first published, those who had hoped for a play that apportioned blame, a political play, were disenchanted, although recognizing that throughout this long dramatic poem, all Genet's coarse tenderness was with the humiliated and tortured Arabs. All the themes of Genet's novels are to be found in this torrential poem which is Elizabethan in its inspiration, its free dramatic structure, its negation of all genres. In addition, it has something of an allegorical puppet-show, Jarry reborn. . . . The play is admirable for its lyricism and its visionary force; it has no lessons or moral. It is an unrelenting tragedy and the final reconciliation of torturers and victims is in no way Christian, it is rather a mocking liturgy of nothingness.

Renée Saurel, *Temps modernes*, June 1966

In any event Genet has not written a political play. He has not taken sides, except for freedom. . . . It is a chivalrously anarchic play. All that is in question is human misery, the rifts between men whom flesh, hatred, and death bring together.

Jean-Louis Barrault, to Pierre Julien,
L'Aurore, 12 April 1966

The play bears a strong relationship to Genet's *The Blacks* . . . dealing with the conflicts between non-whites and whites, have-nots and an aristocracy, rebels and rulers, natives and colonialists. It is set in revolutionary Algeria . . . placing the story of one native, his incredibly ugly bride, and his extravagant mother against a panorama of rebellion, the military, the French colonial aristocracy, and almost anything else that struck Genet's hallucinatory fancy. . . . As usual, the flamboyance of his concepts is more effective than his playwriting and play construction. . . . His revolutionary polemics are absurd as usual and often self-contradictory.

Martin Gottfried, *Women's Wear Daily*, 13 December 1971

Our theatre would be brought to a halt in front of this work, whose corrosive inspiration as regards our national and revolutionary myths would certainly scandalize both the left and the right. . . . For Jean Genet, revolt loses itself in Revolution. Saïd's experience is purely subjective, ascetic and tragic. It has no value which can be taken up by others. . . . Saïd is the one who refuses history and affirms his own irreducible individuality. . . . Like all Genet's works, the play is founded on a rigorous exaltation of the theatrical lie and its relation to the spectator in the here and now of his contemplation of it. To this extent it is a radical critique of the bourgeois theatre. The work is realist in the very fact that far from rebelling against the de-realizing function of theatre, it uses it in order to turn it back cruelly on the audience, identified as the moral bourgeoisie which holds the power to judge and to condemn in the name of principles which it has given itself in order to be right in the face of all that is foreign to it.

Marc Pierret, *France Observateur*, 14 May 1964

Before being the evocation of the Algerian war seen from the other side . . . his play is a long, slow sequence of heart-rending misery and stomach-turning filth. It requires patience; it is long like a mass or like a counter-mass: but in nearly every scene, at nearly every moment, there is a stunning cry of pain, composed of sombrely beautiful words and gestures, as though M. Genet wanted to go beyond the psychological and the social in order to reach the mythical root of revolt.

Robert Kanters, *Express*, 25 April 1966

[The play is not a new departure into politics: it presents many themes common to earlier works.]

It is not an epic, it is a great dramatic, funereal poem in which the major themes of Genet come together according to a strict order, as confident as that of Bach or Giotto: the liturgy of filth, the celebration of evil, sex, hatred, death, . . . the most scandalous, violent, and lyrical protest, not only against society and its signs but against a failed creation of a God who is an imposter, a scoundrel, a malicious entity, and who no longer sustains the saints and their quest. . . . The things and beings in *The Screens* form a theatre of shadows. They are what they are only at the very moment they appear. Not even that. The things are only the words which, in the naming, make them appear (that is why the play is an incantation) and the graffiti which represent them. The world like the theatre is no more than a fleeting construction, made of pieces of nothingness, holes and spaces.

Gilles Sandier, *Arts*, 27 April 1966

It has to be said that Genet is little interested in the colonial war, who wins it and what results from it: the universe into which he plunges us is not that of a people in revolt but his own. . . . The universe of the banished; . . . the universe where evil is exalted and becomes the only chance for salvation; . . . the universe of appearances, lies, and deceptions, in the service of destruction and death. . . . In such an inverted world, vice has recourse to pomp; the brothel becomes the privileged site for its splendour and rituals; the glorification of evil demands a complete ceremonial. . . . Rarely has a playwright gone so far in terms of the crudeness of his utterances, the forthrightness of his vocabulary, his obscenity and scatology. In this flow of mud there shine all of a sudden truly successful images; some very beautiful lyrical images stem the tide for a moment; in other passages, the mud bubbles up under the effect of a ferocious and joyous humour. But, in the end, the triviality and the abjectness submerge all else, as though it were necessary to have an overpowering amount of muck-spreading in order that some new hope could blossom.

Jacques Carat, *Preuves*, June 1966

Genet's real engagement with his material, however, is not on the level of political cartoon; instead, he finds in his epic canvas the opportunity to make another of his statements on the purity and beauty of absolute evil. Genet's interest in, and support of, Algerian rebellion is tentative; he reserves his real enthusiasm for Saïd, his anti-hero, whose goal is to transcend all partisanship and to achieve thereby a glorious isolation. . . . A potentially exhilarating play . . . has been bloated and consequently blunted by Genet's elephantine approach. Structureless, the play meanders from incident to incident picking up and abandoning character and situation with arrogant carelessness. The pace is severely retarded by the swollen set speeches, empty rhetorical exercises about the land and the sky and the trees and the human spirit.

Foster Hirsch, *Educational Theatre Journal*, March 1972

The true meaning and value of the play becomes increasingly clear as its political pretext recedes into the past. . . . Genet has not written an epic on rebellion nor a political analysis. . . . The Algerian conflict is but an opportunity to pick up once more the themes of his whole oeuvre: the hypocrisy of society and the sacred power of Evil.

Bertrand Poirot-Delpech, *Le Monde*, 23 April 1966

The Screens is the cry of revolt uttered by the oppressed, the victims of hypocrisy. What Genet is running down is not the army nor the flag, nor memory, nor devotion, nor charity, nor solidarity, nor order, but the rigidity of a limited militarism, the masquerade of the flag, the comedy of memory, the humiliating mercy of the believer, the traps of charity, the cloying of false solidarity and the spider's web of order.

Jacques Pernot, *Signes du temps*, June 1966

Genet's extraordinary Chinese box of fantasies is underway. Each time one strips away a fantasy, another is revealed, then another and another, until underneath one discovers not truth, but an image. . . . It is not necessary for us to try and divine which is the real one, which is reality out of a series of fantasies, for there is no difference. A truer image for

The Screens would be a kaleidoscope, which creates patterns containing their own evocative power and beauty, independent of the raw material used to produce them. . . . .What one retains from the play, overall, is a kaleidoscope of shifting scenes, enclosing splashes of brilliant colour, darts of pain and longing shafts of crude filth and misery, forming and reforming to make new, pressing patterns.

Tom Milne, Encore, July 1964

[The play is its own subject, or, put another way, the experience of the play constitutes its meaning.]

After years of anti-theatre, here is a play where theatre is sovereign. The free-flowing language and attitudes, the outrageous costumes and situations, everything contrives to remind us that we are in the theatre, but also caught in the trap of which Hamlet speaks: was it reality that was theatrical? Dressed in sumptuous rags, made up like Japanese actresses, new Hecubas, new Cassandras appear before us. . . . This wild play, written in the grips of a disorderly inspiration but with a confidence born of tenacious obsession, this play without a subject or a moral is directed principally at our senses. It aims to take our breath away, stifle us in its horror, to lead us to the other side of ourselves. . . . Beyond all Christian inspired morality, it aims to make us confront our victims — those who suffer from our good conscience, our security.

Guy Dumur, Nouvel Observateur, 27 April 1966

The true subject is the play itself, the play condemned to be played but with no hope of coming to an end. . . . Genet embarrasses, aggresses, sullies us. He makes us the witnessess to the dissolution of man before the advent of the theatre. . . . He denies us along with the judges, colonialists, masters, and forbids us from joining him where he is on the other side of all order, in the realm of absolute negation, which contains the negation of negation, or rather the realm of the acceptance of ignominy and the outcast's self-complacency. . . . The mass and the brothel are there, but the sacredness which springs from their union has no depth. It is the sacredness of pure appearance, of fatal dissolution. It is a mistake to see in *The Screens* some sort of fraternity among out-casts, a saintliness of the lower depths, a prostitute charity.

Baroque theatre goes beyond the comic illusion in order to denounce it and to try to reveal the being beyond the appearances, beyond art, beyond theatre. On the contrary, modern drama is swallowed up in invisibility with illusion dead. It is the theatre of Nothingness. But it shows the Nothing.

Alfred Simon, Esprit, Nov. 1966

The Screens: four hours of celebration, an obscene and excessive mass, a flood of words, images and colours, provocation, theatre, beauty. A first impression of bedazzlement and dizziness. . . . The fact is that on leaving the Odéon, you are aware of having received a volley of blows and of having been deliciously exhausted. The result is a sort of remorse, made up of distress and surprise, but also of the unclear belief of having participated in the celebration of something exalted. . . . What has to be recognized in the play is an imagination capable of forging myths, a visionary and a lyrical power which has perhaps no equal today, an implacable and insatiable need for truth. . . . Therefore, in *The Screens*, we have, as in all Genet's work, the multiplying rites, the sacramental rhythm of the action, the signs, the appearances, the masks, the mirrors. The stage explodes and multiplies itself into simultaneous spaces; what is real is undone, whether by taking on a fantastic beauty, whether by opening up into unknown regions, . . . or whether, again, it grows to become fable, or whether it clads itself in irony and farce. Everything is at the service of the ceremonial.

Robert Abirached, *Nouvelle Revue française*, 1 June 1966

The scenes are scattered, confused, frightening, absurd, and ultimately no more nefarious than a nightmare. The play's very explosion is its meaning. . . . [Genet's] scorn is all-embracing; it aims at universal devastation. The agony within him and the residue of a profoundly Gallic cultural heritage are wrenched from him in immense gusts of grotesque laughter. . . . Genet flagellates himself and us into a new purity through the excess and sullied grandiloquence of his derision.

Harold Clurman, *Nation*, 27 Dec. 1971

[Epic, documentary, liturgical, sacramental, ceremonial, ritualistic, baroque: the adjectives employed to try and capture this work proliferate. It is at one and the same time a modern form of Elizabethan or classical theatre, or a western version of oriental stage drama.]

The Screens represents the opposite of documentary theatre. It is universal theatre, a link with Greek and Chinese forms of theatre. That's what I believe a work of art to be.

Jean-Louis Barrault, to Pierre Julien, *L'Aurore*, 12 April 1966

Genet has rediscovered theatre's roots and its greatness. Thanks to him, the links between the ceremony and liturgy of the ancient theatre and the celebration of the baroque theatre have been re-established.

André Alter, *Témoignage chrétien*, 28 April 1966

The Screens is a play of epic range, of original and devastating theatrical effect, of innumerable details of dramaturgy, language, and stagecraft which add up to a tidal wave of total theatre. But it seems to miss the formal integrity, the inexorable wholeness of Genet's two masterpieces [*The Balcony* and *The Blacks*]. Needless to say it makes everything else on a current stage seem like white boiled potatoes.

> Jack Kroll, *Newsweek*, 27 Dec. 1971

[The effect is either stunning — or soporific.]

Its failure on theatrical grounds is due to its lack of dramatic structure: it has no backbone; its characters are simply the puppets from some demonic dance, lacking all psychological existence; it progresses terrifyingly slowly, four hours of verbiage, repetitions, criss-crossings of themes, a multiplicity of confusing symbols which succeed in losing the audience.

> Gilbert Guilleminault, *L'Aurore*, 23 April 1966

Its gratuitousness, I think, is in the dramatic movement, or rather the interminable succession of scenes which do not develop the story line sufficiently.

> Guy Verdot, *Journal de Genève*, 30 April 1966

More disconcerting, though, is the diffusion that comes of keeping so much. The evening is intended as a mosaic; but even a mosaic needs strong lines that can be seen by stepping just a little back. . . . Figures suddenly become important without ever having been identified for us; others we readily recognize seem to shiver and grow vague. The dramatic equation is never stable. Nor is it at any single time truly powerful. We are never riveted, never thunderstruck, never fully focused, never engrossed. We are interested somewhat; boredom is not the issue, . . . we are mainly spectators at an inventive but overladen puppet-show, willing enough to try and work out the author's thesis, welcoming the thought that at some future time we shall be free to go home.

> Walter Kerr, *New York Times*, 19 Dec. 1971

Moreover we were searching for scandal and it was boredom that we found, a dull, heavy boredom, equal to the obscenity; a tenacious, soporific boredom which takes any idea of protest away and even stops you from leaving the seat in which you are dozing.

> Jean Vigneron, *La Croix*, 23 April 1966

It is a far from easy play; it eludes even as it entertains. It is comprehensible — even enjoyable — scene by scene, yet *in toto* it puzzles and confuses, and its ultimate statements seem grim.

Haskel Frankel, *National Observer*, 25 Dec. 1971

You can leave *The Screens* after a quarter of an hour. Any later and it is too late. You are bound, enchanted, and you cry out only as the rape is committed, a rape which was seen to be coming, but nobody has been able to stop. For Genet's work is a rape perpetrated against us, our morality, our honour, faith, and those who cry out are not alone in feeling its searing heat. Is it theatre? No. Or if it is, what is known as theatre does not exist. It is better to call it a ceremony, an atrocious and splendid ceremony, a blasphemous and pathetic liturgy, a black mass and prayer for man, totally denuded and stripped bare to the depths of his misery, body and soul.

Le Promeneur de la scène, *Gazette de Lausanne*, 7 May 1966

[Of the directors, Roger Blin had the best opportunity to understand Genet's intentions, but the creation of this type of beauty posed problems for actors.]

Genet conceives theatre as fundamentally a celebration, a ceremony which moves towards the baroque with heavily made-up masks and characters contrasting with the realism of the costumes. . . . His style is realistic at the outset, the first words are an everyday enumeration, but as they progress, they grow, become louder, take off from reality and turn towards madness, calling the whole world, the cosmos, the stars into question in his crucible.

Roger Blin, *Entretiens sur le théâtre*, Sept. 1966

Certainly there are lots of meanings but the play has no desired message. Genet does not expect nor want to be believed, to be followed. He only wants to create beauty.

What attracts me theatrically to this play is that it is a deliberately anti-realist statement, seeking a truth of another sort, proving that everything can be attempted and have meaning outside realism. The most precious aspect of *The Screens* is that the words are comic but the whole is tragic: it's a tragedy which uses the language of burlesque.

Roger Blin, *Le Monde*, 16 April 1966

The images, both verbal and visual, emerge from the necessity of the people in action, as, with great energy, they create and build their world out of nothing. Such an approach is not easily available to the English actor. With some exceptions, he still sees himself as an interpreter. . . . Neither his history nor his social identity evolve in him a responsibility and commitment to action, imaginative and political. Because of his own background and experience he is ill-equipped to deal with the emotional and physical demands of a play like *The Screens*.

> Walter Donohue, *Theatre Quarterly*, Feb.-April 1974

[As for the author, he has left detailed comments on the play and its performance.]

Therefore the actors and actresses must be induced to put aside cleverness and to involve the most secret depths of their being; they must be made to accept difficult endeavours, admirable gestures which however have no relation to those they employ in their daily lives. If we maintain that life and the stage are opposites, it is because we strongly suspect that the stage is a site closely akin to death, a place where all liberties are possible.

My play is not an apologia for treason. It takes place in a realm where morality is replaced by the aesthetics of the stage.

People say that plays are generally supposed to have a meaning: not this one. It's a celebration whose elements are disparate, it is the celebration of nothingness.

The point . . . is not to situate too precisely in time a play which is a masquerade.

[Genet's admiration of Blin's work was generous.]

In *The Blacks*, the text of which was more carefully prepared as to its effect, your work amazed me less. In any case, it seems to me that I was as much responsible for its success as you were. In *The Screens*, the full credit goes to you. If I had thought the play could be performed, I would have made it more beautiful — or a complete failure. Without touching it, you have taken it and made it light. It's very beautiful. You have my friendship, and admiration.

> Jean Genet, 'Letters to Roger Blin', in
> *Reflections on the Theatre*, trans. Richard Seaver
> (London: Faber, 1972)

Elle

Written: 1955, also called *Le Pape*; plans to publish it with *Les Nègres*
   were abandoned because of their differences.
First performance: Festival de Parme, 26 April 1989.
Publication: Décines: L'Arbalète, 1989.

This one-act play has affinities with Le Balcon, *which Genet was
revising at the time of its composition. The text is complete
except for one speech by the Pope (the* Elle *of the title). It is set
in an anti-chamber of a papal palace where a photographer has
come to take an official portrait of the Pope for distribution
throughout the world. Running through the dialogue, initially
between the photographer and a papal attendant, and then
between the photographer and the Pope, are the themes of
image, symbol, and existence. Through five set speeches, or
canticles (two delivered by the Pope — a third is not extant —
and two briefly summarized by the attendant), the Pope expresses
his anxieties: the shrivelling of the self in the pursuit of an
Image; the realization that the much-coveted Image is but a
reflection of others' self-absorption; the possibility of replacing
the Image by a symbolic object; the solitude of the Image holder
who has no Image to adore; and the impossibility of throwing off
the Image to rediscover the original, authentic self. These themes
are treated with irreverent humour rather than vitriolic irony;
the language is devoid of the crude savagery of other plays. For
example, the Pope is propelled on roller-skates so that he can
float on and off stage like an angel; he is bare-bottomed because
his public image is always frontal; in an amusing twist, a lump
of sugar becomes his presence, which people can ingest in their
tea and coffee.*

b: Unpublished Plays

Splendid's/Frolic's

Written: 1945-48; this text changed names and was reportedly destroyed in 1952 (see below). It is *unperformed*, although there were announcements of imminent productions in 1952 and 1957, and also *unpublished*, although announced as forthcoming in 1989 by Marc Barbezat of L'Arbalète.

Variously described as a two-act or three-act play, this work shares the underground, criminal world of the novels and Deathwatch. *A group of gangsters are trapped on a rooftop with their dead, kidnapped victim, the daughter of the chief of police. In order to assure the police of her supposed safety, the gang leader dresses up as the young girl. This act of transvestism causes him to lose his status in the gang and he is shot by the second in command.*

Les Fous

Written: Sept. 1957. *Publication* was announced by Marc Barbezat of L'Arbalète in 1989: this publisher has held the contract on this unknown work since 1958, Genet having given permission for its posthumous publication.

La Fée

Written: 1963 or earlier. *Publication* was announced by Marc Barbezat in 1989, under the same conditions as *Les Fous*.

c: Lost Plays

Héliogabale

Reputedly *written* in manuscript form in 1942, inspired by Marais'
performance in *Britannicus*, this would have been Genet's first
dramatic text. Genet wished to write another emperor role for Marais,
who was evidently not interested in the project. The manuscript has
not been traced.

Le Guerrier nu

Written: 1944 or earlier, this unknown and untraced play is mentioned in
correspondence between Genet and Marc Barbezat in March 1944.

Don Juan

Written: 1945 or earlier, this unknown and untraced play is mentioned in
correspondence between Genet and Barbezat in November 1945.

a: Ballet and Mime

Adame Miroir

Written: 1948
First performed: Théâtre de Marigny, 31 May 1948
  (choreography: Janine Charrat, to music by Darius
  Milhaud; dir. Roland Petit).
Publication: Paris: Heugel, 1948. *Translation:* none known.

---

*The action of the ballet concerns a sailor who finds and
dances with his reflection until a domino breaks in and
kills the sailor. The domino returns to dance with the
Image, but reveals himself now to be the murdered
sailor as the Image assumes the appearance of the
domino. They pursue each other until the sailor
disappears through a mirror to leave the domino face to
face with his own image. At the end, he vanishes
through a double mirror at the back of the stage,
holding the sailor's beret, the only sign of the struggle.*

The programme offered only a cryptic note stating that the
observer must find his own meaning for this fantasy, in which
a young man in sailor uniform, wandering in a hall of mirrors,
is joined by his own reflection. They dance together in
identical movement, until both are destroyed by a hooded
figure in purple. This is the sort of ballet which provokes a
great deal of discussion among those people who insist upon
knowing, gesture for word, word for gesture, exactly 'what it
all means'.

Lillian Moore, Dance Magazine, Jan. 1949

The Maids *was made into a ballet by Herbert Ross to music by
Milhaud in May 1957, and* Our Lady of the Flowers *formed
the basis for Lindsay Kemp's much performed and adapted*
Flowers: a Pantomime for Jean Genet, *created in 1974. Genet
had no known involvement in either of these projects.*

b: Film

*Only those film projects to which Genet made a significant artistic
contribution are included here, but Genet and/or his work have inspired
numerous other films, the most important of which are:* The Balcony
(dir. Joseph Strick, 1962); Deathwatch *(dir. Vic Morrow, 1966);* The
Maids *(dir. Christopher Miles, 1974); and* Querelle *(dir. Rainer Werner
Fassbinder, 1982). Further details of Genet's involvement with film can
be found in the study by Jane Giles,* The Cinema of Jean Genet *(London:
British Film Institute, 1991).*

Un Chant d'amour

Released: France, 1950; black and white, silent, 25 minutes (dir. Jean
Genet). The film was banned in France from 1951 to 1974, though it
may have been seen at the Cinémathèque in 1954. Court cases kept it
off the screen in the USA, although it was shown in New York in
March 1964. More recently it has featured at film festivals and
independent cinemas.

Genet's only film — hounded by the censors, unavailable, secret — is
an early and remarkably moving attempt to portray homosexual
passions. Already a classic, it succeeds as perhaps no other film to
intimate the explosive power of frustrated sex; male prisoners in solitary
confinement 'embracing' walls, ramming them in erotic despair with
erect penis, swaying convulsively to auto-erotic lust, kissing their own
bodies and tatoos in sexual frenzy. In a supremely poetic (and visual)
metaphor of sexual deprivation, two prisoners in adjoining cells
symbolically perform fellatio by alternatively blowing or inhaling each
other's cigarette smoke through a straw inserted in a wall opening, while
masturbating. Like all Genet's early work, the entire film is, in effect, a
single onanistic fantasy, filled with desperate frustration and sensuous
nostalgia. In the end, and after many failures, some flowers — painfully
passed from one barred window to the next — are finally caught by the
prisoner in the adjoining cell in a poetic affirmation of love in infinite
imprisonment.

Amos Vogel, *Film as a Subversive Art*
(Weidenfeld and Nicolson, 1974)

Mademoiselle

Released: France and UK, 1965; black and white, 105 minutes (scenario by Jean Genet; dir. Tony Richardson). A scenario bearing the subtitle *Les Feux interdits* was read by Henri Chapier as early as 1951. By 1958 it had reportedly grown to 100 pages.

The schoolmistress of a remote French farming village is a seemingly prim and introverted young spinster, but beneath her calm exterior she is filled with suppressed sexual desires that erupt into secret acts of violence and wanton destruction. Opening floodgates to drown farm stock, setting fire to barns and homes, poisoning the water in drinking fountains for animals, and smashing the nests of field birds, she takes perverse physical pleasure in the havoc she causes. The outraged villagers, needing someone to blame for the series of disasters, turn against a lusty Italian woodcutter, Manou, who has recently moved into the community. . . . Manou is resented by the local men because of the animal magnetism he exerts over women, a magnetism he exploits to the fullest. One day, the schoolmistress, incensed by Manou's indifference to her, lures him into a field and seduces him by crawling on her stomach and licking his hands and boots like a dog. Then, when the orgy is over, she returns to the village, her clothing torn and splattered with mud, and flatly states that Manou raped her. The already mounting anger of the village men now bursts into frenzy and they seek Manou out and stone him to death. Her passions momentarily sated, the schoolmistress accepts the sympathy of her neighbours, packs her few belongings, and leaves the village.

Filmfacts, No. 9 (1966)

Mr. Richardson is poetically dreamy and dreadfully solemn as he unveils these purported mysteries of feminine sexuality, and, amazingly, Miss Moreau somehow preserves her essential dignity through it all. The film has occasional fascinations, but its revelations concerning the destructiveness of the sexually thwarted female come out part lurid sensationalism and part Krafft-Ebing case history.

Hollis Alpert, *Saturday Review*, 27 Aug. 1966

One can only suspect that Tony Richardson and the notoriously sadistic

Jean Genet were out to denigrate and castigate a woman as much as they could in this film. For there is no redeeming quality in the spectacularly vicious female here. She is absorbed by nothing but tangled passion, selfishness and hate. . . . All this, furthermore, is expounded in a lurid, gravely melodramatic manner that is shocking from Mr. Richardson.

Bosley Crowther, *New York Times*, 2 Aug. 1966

Le Bagne

This work, first reported as a film project in 1952, was to have been shot in Rome in 1953. Marc Barbezat had the manuscript of a work bearing this title, now apparently a play, in 1956. In 1965 it was still being worked on. It was announced in 1989 by Marc Barbezat as forthcoming from L'Arbalète.

A young criminal realizes that life in prison can be tolerated only if he maintains his prestige by intimidating his fellow inmates. In order to achieve this end he admits spuriously to the murder of a warder who had had his eye put out by a needle as he spied on cellmates. By assuming this crime, the young criminal gains respect in the eyes of the other prisoners. He goes to his execution as a big shot.

La Nuit venue

Under its original title, *Le Bleu de l'oeil*, this project was begun in 1976. The scenario was written by Genet from an original idea by Mohamed El Katrani, and was to have been co-directed by Genet and Ghislain Uhry. The film was to tell the story of a young Moroccan's journey to France by train and was to treat the theme of racism. The project was abandoned in 1978. The script for the opening scene, still bearing the original title, has appeared in *Les Nègres au Port de la Lune: Genet et les différences* (Paris: La Différence, 1988).

c: Poems

Genet's six published poems all date from the period of his novels. They have received very little attention.

Yet the verse has a continuity of themes with the prose: homosexual love, crime and punishment, apotheosis of the criminal. The same symbolic images are used (roses, jewels, angels, darkness, water, blue, masks, blood, iron). The same persons reappear. . . . But Genet's poetic models held back his development as a poet. They were mostly half a century out of date, and the regular rhyming stanzas he tended to use made it too hard for him to achieve any of the extraordinary combinations of lyricism and slang which characterize his novels.

Edwin Morgan, in *The Theater of Jean Genet: a Casebook*,
ed. Richard N. Coe (New York: Grove, 1970)

d: Fiction and Autobiography

Surprisingly, there has been relatively little serious commentary on Genet's prose writings. Initially published clandestinely, they attracted scant attention, and any notice subsequently given them has tended to consider all the works as one. Early comment highlighted, as Richard Coe has pointed out, Genet's magical style, his place in a continuing tradition of French literature (he is most often compared with Proust and Rimbaud), and the moral dimension of his work which lays bare the hidden recesses of human nature. There was much more comment on the publication of the translations in Britain and the USA.

Our Lady of the Flowers
(Notre-Dame des fleurs)

Written: begun Jan. 1942.

Publication: Sept. 1944, in a private limited edition; another limited
    edition followed (Lyon: Barbezat, 1948); and a revised version was
    included in the *Oeuvres complètes*, Vol. II (Paris: Gallimard, 1951).

Translation: by Bernard Frechtman, Paris: Paul Morihien, 1949 (original
    version); also by Frechtman, New York: Grove, 1963; London:
    Blond, 1964 (revised version).

Our Lady of the Flowers may seem shamelessly immoral. It is not. It is shamelessly aesthetic. It declares itself as a deliberately sexual exercise of the imagination. The writer constitutes himself as a multiple sensory organ. . . . The writing of the book is itself a metaphoric act, a substitute for and a prolongation of sexual self-stimulation. . . . I don't know whether to praise more the language, . . . its daring method of construction, or the endless fertility of its ideas.

Susan Sontag, *Sunday Herald Tribune*, 6 Oct. 1963

Miracle of the Rose (Miracle de la rose)

Written: begun 1943, under title *Le Mystère des enfants des anges.*
Publication: in a limited edition, Lyon: Barbezat, 1946; revised version in *Oeuvres Complètes*, Vol. II (Paris: Gallimard, 1951).
Translation: by Bernard Frechtman, New York: Grove; London: Blond, 1965.

Genet's whole effort in this book is to reassemble a shattered and fragmented paradise. This is the immemorial motif that lies at the centre of his art, making him the romantic he is — the only first-rate romantic genius of post-war world literature. . . . [*Miracle*] is a monument to a peculiarly virile kind of energy: an act of transgression and completeness that puts before 'us' the determination to create itself autonomously, to stand on its own terms. It begins in rebellion and ends as a work of self-contained beauty which no longer needs 'us' to give it meaning.

Stephen Koch, *The Nation*, 12 June 1967

Funeral Rites (Pompes funèbres)

Written: begun in 1943, under title *Spectre du coeur*; reportedly destroyed and begun again.
Publication: two limited editions of the original version were in existence by 1948, one probably published by Paul Morihien in Paris; a revised version appeared in *Oeuvres complètes*, Vol. III (Paris: Gallimard, 1953).
Translation: by Bernard Frechtman, New York: Grove; London: Blond, 1969.

Predictably, the book is a free-flowing series of homosexual encounters and fantasies written in a dense style with allusions and puns, many of which need awkward footnotes from the translator. Genet's people meet one another groin to groin, like a society of disembodied pelvises. The narrative *I* of the novel shifts from character to character, inhabiting each with a kind of lovingly brutal sexuality, simultaneously celebrating the violence of war and the violence of entry and orgasm. The occupation of France comes to signify a sexual as well as a political situation; a perverse world reverberating to the cries of pain and pleasure in anal intercourse. Yet in the face of all the real and fantasized atrocities in the book, the tone of Genet's writing is extraordinarily that of the shocked, pious Catholic petit-bourgeois. The world of *Funeral Rites* is recorded with the dour accuracy of an account-book; and beneath some of the verbal antics of the surface one senses a simple horror at a universe in which the act of private perversity can never rival the wholesale bestiality of history itself.

Jonathan Raban, *New Statesman*, 3 Oct. 1969

Querelle of Brest (Querelle de Brest)

Written: 1945-46.

Publication: at least two limited editons were in circulation in 1947, probably published by Paul Morihien in Paris; a revised version appeared in *Oeuvres complètes*, Vol. III (Paris: Gallimard, 1953).

Translation: by Gregory Streatham, London: Blond, 1966; New York: Grove, 1967.

In *Our Lady of the Flowers* the mythological side of Genet's genius, that faculty which could find grandeur in thieves' slang or in a queen's decision to crown herself with her own dentures, was the stronger half. In *Querelle* the mythological and the analytical powers seem to be in perfect balance. By mythologizing his hero, Genet makes him as bright as not just a star but an entire constellation; through analysis, Genet delineates the subtle dynamics that relate one character to another.

Edmund White, *New York Times Book Review*, 8 Sept. 1974

The Thief's Journal (Journal du voleur)

Written: begun in 1945.

Publication: a limited edition was in circulation in 1948 or 1949 (no publishing details); a slightly revised version, Paris: Gallimard, 1949.
Translation: by Bernard Frechtman, Paris: Olympia Press, 1954 (first version); New York: Grove, 1964; London: Blond, 1965 (revised version).

Actually, Genet's *The Thief's Journal* is also an act of gigantic courage, though in this case of the purely spiritual order. His premises are perhaps among the least likely to lead to anything other than a prime specimen of pretentious satanism. He starts by standing all received morality indecorously on its head. His gods are theft, buggery, treachery, self-prostitution, self-immolation. But what he makes of them is so much not a willed work, and is so much a lived one, that one can only range the *Journal* with the writings of the greatest mystics. The slum, the ponce, the filthy cell, these too are a path of the negative way. The author has disappeared entirely into his own existence. It is a great work of art, and as exact an example of how to do it, of how to create the novel of no return, as Norman Mailer's late egotistical trumpetings are the opposite.

Helen Corke, *The Listener*, 13 May 1965

Prisoner of Love (Un Captif amoureux)

Written: begun in final form, 1983.
Publication: Paris: Gallimard, 1986.
Translation: by Barbara Bray, London: Picador, 1989.

Is it a report, a fictionalized account, a discursive meditation, a long prose poem? Whatever it is, a rational or logical reading must be guarded against: throughout its whole length this text operates an inversion of values which forces the reading process into a disconcerting and almost fantastic realm. One next to another we encounter scenes, reflections, places, people who sometimes become blurred and disappear and on other occasions become flesh and blood and refuse to leave us: they begin by being contingent but they finally force the reader's resistance and tame it.

Annie Cohen-Solal, *Nouvel Observateur*, 23 May 1986

e: The 'Great Work'

In Saint Genet *(1952), Sartre announced a major new work by Genet. This work had various working titles (e.g.* Enfers, La Mort*), but it was never completed. Genet was reported to be working on the text for ten years or so. It was to be in two volumes: the first of prose; the second possibly a cycle of seven plays, including* La Mère *(an alternative title for* Les Paravents*).* Fragments *(1954) is perhaps a draft of a part of the first volume. It treats homosexuality as well as examining the possibility of aesthetics as a basis or substitute for morality.*

f: Art Criticism

Genet has written on Léonor Fini (1950), Alberto Giacometti (1957), and Rembrandt (1959, 1964, 1967), as well as a performance artist in Le Funambule *(1958). The essays are as much about Genet's self-perception as an artist and his understanding of the artistic process as their subjects, sharing a common preoccupation with moral and physical solitude, the manipulation of form, ceremonial, and death. Above all, Genet admires the way in which the artists in question have disappeared behind their works and thus achieved anonymity.*

g: Political Writings

After 1967 most of Genet's occasional writing was concerned with socio-political themes. Involved in the student unrest in Paris in 1968, he was in the same year writing bitingly anti-American eye-witness pieces in response to the Chicago Democratic convention. A series of articles for the underground press flowed from his involvement with Angela Davis and the Black Panthers, culminating in his preface for L'Assassinat de Georges Jackson *(Gallimard, 1971). In Europe, his support for the German terrorist Baader-Meinhoff group took the form of a preface to the prison letters of Ulrike Meinhoff (Maspéro, 1977). And in France itself, he embraced the cause of immigrant workers in newspaper articles on their condition and in oblique criticism of the notion of nationhood which underpinned colonialist attitudes (1974, 1977). From the early 'seventies onwards he was involved with the Palestinian cause; his experiences found literary expression in* Le Captif amoureux *(1986).*

[Genet's seminal statement on theatre was made in the 'Lettre à Jean-Jacques Pauvert', which prefaced the 1954 edition of *Les Bonnes*.]

On a stage very similar to ours, on a platform, the end of a meal was being enacted. From this single fact which is now almost totally forgotten, has sprung the highest form of modern drama, performed every day for two thousand years in the sacrifice of the Mass. Its origins disappear beneath the profusion of ornaments and symbols which still overwhelm us. In the most everyday guise — a crust of bread — we eat a god. I know of nothing more theatrically effective than the elevation of the host. . . . A performance that does not touch my soul is purposeless. It is purposeless if I do not believe in what I see, which will come to an end — which will never have been — when the curtain falls. One of the functions of art must be to substitute the efficacy of beauty for religious faith. That beauty must have at least the power of a poem, that is to say of a crime.

I have spoken of communion. Modern theatre is a diversion. On rare occasions it happens to be a quality diversion. The word itself suggests the idea of dispersion. I am not aware of a play which unites the spectators for even as much as an hour. On the contrary, plays isolate them even more. Yet, Sartre told me he had experienced religious fervour during a theatrical performance: in a prison camp, at Christmas, some soldiers, who were mediocre actors, had put on a play about some theme or other — revolt, captivity, courage? — and the distant Homeland was suddenly present, not on the stage, but in the auditorium. A clandestine theatre which one would come to at night and in a mask, a theatre in the catacombs, could still be possible. All that would be needed would be to discover — or create — the common Enemy, then the Homeland to be protected or regained. I don't know what theatre will become in a socialist world; I have a better idea what it would be for the Mau-Mau, but in our western world, which is ever more marked with death and moving towards it, theatre can only be a refinement of a reflection of a play of a play, a reflection of a reflection which a ceremonious performance would make exquisite and close to invisibility. If we have chosen to watch ourselves die in delectation, we have to pursue rigorously and array the funeral symbols. Or choose to live and discover the Enemy. For me, the Enemy will never be anywhere; the

Homeland, be it abstract or interior, will no longer exist. If I am moved, it will be by the nostalgic recollection of what it was. Only a theatre of shadows could still move me. A young writer told me that he had seen five or six young children playing war in a park. They had divided themselves up into two troops and were preparing to attack. Night, they said, was drawing near. But it was midday overhead. They decided therefore that one of them would be Night. The youngest, the most frail amongst them, became the most essential, as the master of the battle. He was the Hour, the Moment, the Ineluctable. It seems that he was advancing from a long way off, with the calmness of an inevitable event, but weighed down by the sadness and ceremony of approaching night. As he drew near, the others, the soldiers, became nervous, uneasy. . . . The boy was coming too soon for their liking. He was before his time: the troops and the commanders were all of one accord in deciding to do away with Night, who became a foot soldier. . . . It is on the basis of this formula alone that theatre can delight me.

> Genet, 'Lettre à Jean-Jacques Pauvert', in
> *Les Bonnes* (Sceaux: Pauvert, 1954)

[These early thoughts find echoes in Genet's essay of 1967, 'L'Etrange mot de . . .', which ranges more widely into cultural criticism.]

Going back as far as we can to the very origins of theatre, it would seem that, in addition to its essential function, each play was crammed with concerns deriving from politics, religion, morality, or what have you, transforming the dramatic action into a didactic means of expression.

Perhaps . . . perhaps television and movies will perform better the role of education; then the theatre will find itself emptied, perhaps cleansed, of whatever encumbered it; perhaps it may shine brightly with its own inherent quality or qualities — which perhaps remains, or remain, to be discovered.

If they are able to accept the idea . . . that the theatre cannot compete with the extraordinary means which television and cinema have at their disposal, then those who write for the theatre will discover the virtues inherent in theatre, virtues which, perhaps, derive only from myth.

Politics, history, classical physiological demonstrations, an evening's light entertainment ought to give way to something else which I don't know quite how to describe but which I suspect will be more dazzling. All this dung, all this liquid manure will be eliminated.

I might point out, in passing, that . . . words and situations that are termed vulgar or uncouth hurried to my plays, sought refuge in them where they were granted the right of sanctuary. If my theatre stinks, it is because the other smells so sweet.

But what about the drama? If its origin is some dazzling moment in the author's experience, it is up to him to seize this lightning and, beginning with the moment of illumination which reveals the void, to arrange a verbal architecture — that is, grammatical and ceremonial — slyly suggesting from this void some semblance is snatched which reveals the void.

Not having given a great deal of thought to theatre, I still have the feeling that what matters is not to multiply the number of performances so that the greatest number of spectators can profit (?) from them, but rather to work so that the attempts — which are called rehearsals — culminate in one performance of such great intensity and brilliance that, by the spark it will have ignited in each spectator, it will suffice to illuminate those who did not take part in it, and make them uneasy.

Among other things, the goal of the theatre is to take us outside the limits of what is generally referred to as 'historical' time but which is really theological. The moment the theatrical event begins, the time which will elapse no longer belongs to any calibrated calendar. It transcends the christian era as it does the revolutionary era. Even if that time which is called 'historical' . . . does not disappear completely from the spectators' consciousness, another time, which each spectator lives to the full, then unfolds, and as it has neither beginning nor end, it destroys the historical conventions necessitated by social life, and at the same time destroys social conventions as well, not for the sake of just any disorder but neither for the sake of a liberation — the theatrical event being suspended, outside of historical time, on its own dramatic time — it is for the sake of a vertiginous liberation.

It's possible that the theatrical art will disappear one day. That's a notion you have to accept. If someday man's activities were to become revolutionary, day after day, the theatre would have no place in life. Or if a dulling of the mind were to someday lead man to daydreaming, then the theatre would also die.

Genet, 'The Strange Word *Urb*. . .', in
Reflections on the Theatre, trans. Richard Seaver
(London: Faber, 1972)

a: Primary Sources

In French

Details of Genet's writing not given in the text can be found in the 'Bibliographical Sources' listed on page 96, below. Most of the major works have been published by Gallimard (Paris) in the collection entitled *Les Oeuvres complètes*, as follows:

Vol I (1951): Jean-Paul Sartre, *Saint Genet: comédien et martyr*.

Vol. II (1951): *Notre-Dame des fleurs, Le Condamné à mort, Miracle de la rose, Un Chant d'amour*.

Vol. III (1953): *Pompes funèbres, Le Pêcheur du Souquet, Querelle de Brest*.

Vol. IV (1968): *L'Etrange mot d'. . . , Ce qui est resté d'un Rembrandt déchiré en petits carrés . . . , Le Balcon, Les Bonnes, Haute surveillance, Lettres à Roger Blin, Comment jouer* Les Bonnes, *Comment jouer* Le Balcon.

Vol. V (1979): *Le Funambule, Le Secret de Rembrandt, L'Atelier d'Alberto Giacometti, Les Nègres, Les Paravents, L'Enfant criminel*.

See also the *Lettres à Olga et Marc Barbezat* (Décines: L'Arbalète, 1988).

In English Translation

All the plays in the editions below were translated by Bernard Frechtman.

Deathwatch. London: Faber and Faber, 1966.
The Maids. London: Faber and Faber, 1963.
The Balcony. Revised version, London: Faber and Faber, 1978.
The Blacks: a Clown Show. London: Faber and Faber, 1967.
The Screens. London: Faber and Faber, 1987.

See also Genet's *Reflections on the Theatre and Other Writings*, translated by Richard Seaver (London: Faber and Faber, 1972). This includes 'Letters to Roger Blin', on his production of *The Screens* in 1966, 'The Strange Word Urb', and 'What Remained of a Rembrandt'.

b: Secondary Sources

Biographical Studies

Albert Dichy and Pascal Fouché, *Jean Genet: Essai de chronologie, 1910-1944* (Paris: Bibliothèque de la littérature contemporaine, 1988).

Jean Bernard Moraly, *La Vie écrite* (Paris: La Différence, 1988).

Jean-Paul Sartre, *Saint Genet: comédien et martyr* (Paris: Gallimard, 1951); translated by Bernard Frechtman as *Saint Genet: Actor and Martyr* (London: W. H. Allen, 1964).

Harry E. Stewart and Rob Roy McGregor, *Jean Genet: a Biography of Deceit* (London: Peter Lang, 1989).

Full-Length General Studies

Gisèle A. Child Bickle, *Jean Genet: criminalité et transcendance* (Saratoga, Calif.: Anma Libri, 1987).

Claude Bonnefroy, *Genet* (Paris: Editions universitaires, 1965).

Peter Brooks and Joseph Heilpern, eds., *Genet: a Collection of Critical Essays* (New York: Prentice-Hall, 1979).

Richard N. Coe, *The Vision of Jean Genet* (London: Owen, 1968).

Tom F. Driver, *Jean Genet* (New York: Columbia University Press, 1966).

Bettina L. Knapp, *Jean Genet* (New York: Twayne, 1968).

Jean-Marie Magnan, *Essai sur Jean Genet* (Paris: Seghers, 1971).

Arnaud Malgorn, *Jean Genet* (Paris: La Manufacture, 1988).

Joseph McMahon, *The Imagination of Jean Genet* (New Haven: Yale University Press, 1963).

Camille Naish, *A Genetic Approach to Structures in the Work of Jean Genet* (Cambridge, Mass.: Harvard University Press, 1978).

Philip Thody, *Jean Genet: a Study of His Novels and Plays* (London: Hamilton, 1968).

Studies of the Plays

Odette Aslan, *Jean Genet* (Paris: Seghers, 1973).

Robert Brustein, *The Theatre of Revolt: an Approach to Modern Drama* (London: Methuen, 1965), pp. 361-411.

Lewis T. Cetta, *Profane Play, Ritual, and Jean Genet: a Study of His Drama* (Alabama: University of Alabama Press, 1974).

Richard N. Coe, ed., *The Theater of Jean Genet: a Casebook* (New York: Grove, 1970).

Bernard Dort, 'Genet ou le combat avec le théâtre', *Temps modernes*, No. 247 (Dec. 1966), p. 1094-9.

Bernard Dort, 'Genet's Make-Believe', *Encore*, No. 31 (May-June 1961), p. 13-17.

Martin Esslin, *The Theatre of the Absurd* (Garden City, New York: Doubleday, 1969), p. 166-97.

Lucien Goldmann, 'The Theatre of Jean Genet: a Sociological Study', *The Drama Review*, XII, No. 2 (Winter 1968), p. 51-61.

David I. Grossvogel, *The Blasphemers: the Theater of Brecht, Ionesco, Beckett, Genet* (Cornell: Cornell University Press, 1965), p. 135-74.

Jacques Guicharnaud, *Modern French Theatre: from Giraudoux to Beckett* (New Haven: Yale University Press, 1967), p. 259-77.

Jean Bernard Moraly, *L'Oeuvre impossible* (Paris: La Différence, 1989).

Obliques, No.2 (1972), p. 1-85.

Leornard C. Pronko, *Avant-Garde: Experimental Theater in France* (Cambridge: Cambridge University Press, 1962), p. 140-53.

Jeannette L. Savona, *Jean Genet* (London: Macmillan, 1983).

George Wellwarth, *The Theater of Protest and Paradox: Developments in the Avant-Garde Drama* (New York: New York University Press, 1971), p. 127-48.

Deathwatch

Maggie Megaw, 'Jean Genet's *Haute surveillance*: a Study of the Manuscripts', *Library Chronicle (Austin)*, XIV (1980), p. 67- 99.

Harry E. Stewart, 'In Defence of Lefranc as a "Hero" of *Haute surveillance*', *French Review*, XLV, No. 2 (Dec. 1971), p. 365-72.

The Maids

Denis Bablet and Jean Jacquot, '*Les Bonnes* de Jean Genet dans la mise en scène de Victor Garcia', in *Les Voies de la création théâtrale*, Vol. IV (Paris: CNRS, 1975), p. 103-315.

Anne C. Murch, 'Genet, Triana, Kopit: Ritual as Danse Macabre', *Modern Drama*, XV, No. 4 (1973), p. 369-91.

Oreste F. Pucciani, 'Tragedy, Genet, and *The Maids*', *Tulane Drama Review*, VII, No. 3 (1963), p. 42-59.

R. A. Zimbardo, 'Genet's Black Mass', *Modern Drama*, VIII, No. 3 (1965), p. 247-58.

The Balcony

Albert Bermel, 'The Society as a Brothel: Genet's Satire in *The Balcony*', *Modern Drama*, XIX, No. 3 (1976), p. 265-80.

Albert C. Chesneau, 'Idée de révolution et principe de reversabilité dans *Le Balcon* et *Les Nègres* de Jean Genet', *PMLA*, LXXXVIII, No. 5 (1973), p. 1137-45.

Ruth Escobar, '*The Balcony*: a Photo Portfolio', *Performance*, I, No.1 (1971), p. 98-109.

Gisèle Feal, '*Le Balcon* de Genet ou le culte matriarchal: une interprétation mythique', *French Review*, XLVIII, No. 5 (1975), p. 897-907.

Lucien Goldmann, 'Genet's *The Balcony*: a Realist Play', *Praxis*, No. 4 (1978), p. 123-31.

David H. Walker, 'Revolution and Revisions in Genet's *Le Balcon*', *Modern Languages Review*, LXXIX, No. 4 (1984), p. 817-30.

The Blacks

Una Chaudhuri, 'The Politics of Theater: Play, Deceit, and Threat in Genet's *The Blacks*', *Modern Drama*, XXIX, No. 3 (1985), p. 362-75.

Bernard F. Dukore, '*The Blacks*; the Rite of Revenge and the Reality of the Double Negative', *Western Speech*, XXVII, No. 3 (1963), p. 133-41.

Allan Francovich, 'Genet's Theatre of Possession', *The Drama Review*, XIV, No. 1 (1969), p. 25-45.

Lucien Goldmann, *et al.*, 'Dans les 25 premiers [*sic*] répliques microstructures des *Nègres* de Jean Genet', *Modern Language Notes*, LXXXII, No. 5 (1967), p. 531-48.

Duncan Graham-White, 'Jean Genet and the Psychology of Colonialism', *Comparative Drama*, IV, No. 3 (1970), p. 208-16.

George B. MacDonald, '*The Blacks* and the Ritual Theatre', *Humanities*, XXI, No. 2 (1962), p. 32-44.

Graham Dunstan Martin, 'Racism in Genet's *Les Nègres*', *Modern Language Review*, LXX, No. 3 (1975), p. 517-25.

Anne C. Murch, 'Je mime donc je suis: *Les Nègres* de Jean Genet', *Revue des Sciences Humaines*, No. 150 (1973), p. 249-59.

Les Nègres au Port de la Lune: Genet et les différences (Paris: La Différence, 1988).

Michèle Piemme, 'Les espaces scéniques et dramaturgiques dans *Les Nègres* de Jean Genet', *Marche Romane*, XX, No.3 (1970), p. 39-52.

Jeannette L. Savona, '*The Blacks* by Jean Genet: a Dimensional Approach', *Australian Journal of French Studies*, X, No. 2 (1973), p. 203-22.

W. F. Sohlich, 'Genet's *The Blacks* and *The Screens*: Dialectic of Refusal and Revolutionary Consciousness', *Comparative Drama*, X, No. 3 (1976), p. 216-34.

Homer D. Swander, 'Shakespeare and the Harlem Clowns: Illusion and Comic Form in Genet's *The Blacks*', Yale Review, LV, No. 2 (1965), p. 209-26.

Susan Taubes, 'The White Mask Falls', *Tulane Drama Review*, VII, No. 3 (1963), p. 85-92.

Richard C. Webb, 'Ritual, Theatre, and Jean Genet's *The Blacks*', *Theatre Journal*, XXXI, No. 4 (1979), p. 443-59.

Michael J. Worton, 'The Temptation of Language in Genet's *Les Nègres*', *French Forum*, III, No. 2 (1978), p. 169-77.

The Screens

Odette Aslan, '*Les Paravents* de Jean Genet', in *Les Voies de la création théâtrale*, Vol. III, ed. Denis Bablet and Jean Jacquot (Paris: CNRS, 1972), p. 11-107.

Odette Aslan, '*Les Paravents*', in *Les Voies de la création théâtrale*, Vol. XIV, ed. Denis Bablet and Jean Jacquot (Paris: CNRS, 1986), p. 292-317.

Walter Donohue, 'Genet's *The Screens* at Bristol', *Theatre Quarterly*, IV, No. 1 (1974), p. 74-90.

Marc Pierret, 'Genet's New Play: *The Screens*', *Tulane Drama Review*, VII, No. 3 (1963), p. 93-7.

Leornard C. Pronko, 'Jean Genet's *Les Paravents*', *L'Esprit Créateur*, II, No. 4 (1962), p. 181-8.

Margaret Scarborough, 'The Radical Idealism of *The Screens*', *Modern Drama*, XV, No.4 (1973), p. 355-68.

Bibliographical Sources

Richard N. Coe, 'Jean Genet: a Checklist of His Works in French, English, and German', *Australian Journal of French Studies*, VI, No. 1 (1969), p. 113-30.

Richard N. Coe, 'Unbalanced Opinions: a Study of Jean Genet and the French Critics', *Proceedings of the Leeds Philosophical and Literary Society*, XIV, Part II (1970), p. 27-73.

Richard C. and Suzanne A. Webb, *Jean Genet and his Critics: an Annotated Bibliography, 1943-1980* (Metuchen, N.J.: Scarecrow Press, 1982).